Computer Crime and Business Information

A Practical Guide for Managers

Computer Crime and Business Information

A Practical Guide for Managers

James A. Schweitzer

Elsevier
New York · Amsterdam · Oxford

Elsevier Science Publishing Co., Inc.
52 Vanderbilt Avenue, New York, New York 10017

Distributors outside the United States and Canada:

Elsevier Science Publishers B.V.
P.O. Box 211, 1000 AE Amsterdam, The Netherlands

Library of Congress Cataloging in Publication Data

Schweitzer, James A., 1929–
    Computer crime and business information.

    Bibliography: p.
    Includes index.
    1. Information resources management.   2. Electronic data processing
    departments—Security measures.   3. Computer crimes.   I. Title.
T58.64.S39   1986   658.4'78   85-13632
ISBN 0-444-00972-8

Current printing (last digit):
10 9 8 7 6 5 4 3 2 1

Manufactured in the United States of America

To
John, Paul, Donna, David,
Chris, Marybeth, and Dan

Contents

Preface

In August 1977 I was asked to develop and implement a security program for electronic information at the Xerox Corporation, a worldwide manufacturer of office systems. Since the task was defined in very general terms, I had the opportunity to set up a management process rather than merely address a set of issues. My experience in systems design, data-center management, and the United States Air Force over a period of twenty-four years gave me a fairly comprehensive viewpoint.

In innumerable discussions, visits, reviews, and professional contacts since I've found that most business managers have a real concern about "computer security" but fail to see the issue in its true context. As a result, many address the matter with short-range, narrowly focused decisions; the resulting programs fail to meet today's business needs for information quality. Decisions that address only the security issue are ineffective in the current high-tech/high competition environment.

The correct solution is one that envisions computer security as a subset of the much broader management issue of information resource management. In this book we will see why information is now the most critical of assets; how managers should value information in preparation for managing it like other resources; and how we can ensure information quality and availability only through proper management and control. Figure P.1 illustrates in graphic form this management challenge of the "information age."

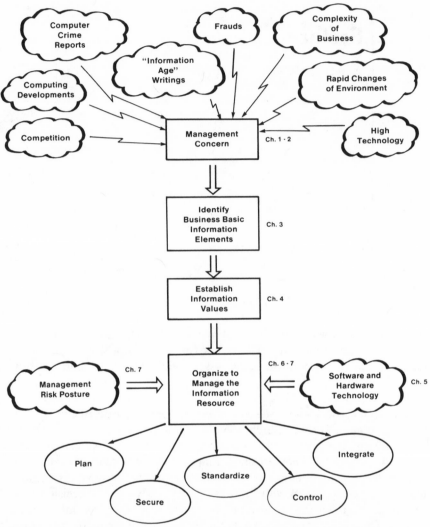

Figure P.1 A macro view of the Information Resource Management challenge.

Acknowledgment

Once again Henry Wold has assisted me by reading my original messy manuscript and making invaluable suggestions on organization and content. This is the third book for which Henry has served as the "honest man" in helping me straighten out my thoughts on a complex subject.

I | Computer-Related Crime and the Business Information Resource

1 | The Information Age

Information systems are spreading throughout the public and private sectors of the United States and the world. The question is no longer whether or not we should have networks, but how we could establish them to maximize the effectiveness and efficiency in a manner which will insure their use for public good.

—Domestic Council on the Right To Privacy (1973)

The information age is here. Information has become a critical resource. Important benefits will be gained by those who recognize the changing times and adapt well. But there are also severe risks—especially for managers who fail to take proper precautions, as demonstrated by these stories:

Three men who, police said, stumbled upon a freak combination of input codes that allowed them to make as many as 250 unrecorded withdrawals in one night, have been charged with stealing nearly $40,000 from automated teller machines. (*Computerworld*, October 8, 1984)

The New York Times (August 14, 1983) reported that some "hackers" had gotten into computer files belonging to a nuclear weapons laboratory.

An employee of a Federal Reserve Bank had used access codes to illicitly obtain money supply figures, intending to use the data to benefit customers at a brokerage firm. (*Management Information Systems Week*, January 12, 1983)

These problems occurred not because of technology, but because managers failed to institute proper control actions.

The human race has progressed through a series of ages that were the product of its development and use of tools, among them the agricultural age, the industrial age, and now the information age. Early in the industrial age invention of the cotton gin and knitting machinery, closely tied to the advent of the steam engine and the railroad, meant that handwork and the "cottage industry" were doomed. Products could be generated in quantity, with standard parts and consistent quality. Henry Ford, of course, immediately comes to mind as one of the first of the great industrial innovators.

With mass production industry required extensive recordkeeping, most done by hand; today's vast multinational corporations were unknown because early twentieth-century transportation and communication simply could not provide for the management and control of far-flung operations.

Even fifty years ago our present seemingly endless quest for information and information-related services did not exist, because the means for high-volume information collection and processing were not available. The introduction of punched-card processing (first used by the U.S. census bureau) and then the development of computing during World War II provided both the impetus and the means for the information age.

The replacement of skilled hand labor by machinery effected the transition from the agricultural age to the industrial age; now we are seeing the replacement of human machine-use skills by robots, the use of tele-conferencing as a substitute for travel, and the delivery of computing power to the personal level as a replacement for mechanical, paper-based personal tools.

Large numbers of people are now trained to handle electronic forms of information and work full time at it—computer scientists, office workers, engineers, accountants, newspaper staff, and telephone technicians. Some of these jobs have been around for a long time; others are relatively new. The important thing is that all increasingly use computers, often personal workstation computers, allowing them to retrieve, generate, and process volumes of information unthinkable in an earlier, simpler age.

John Naisbitt describes the unheralded arrival of the information age in 1956–1957 in his book MEGATRENDS (1982). Among the important effects of this successor to the industrial age are:

The increasing importance of information as a primary business resource.

Recognition of the cost of information as a major business investment (by 1990, by one expert's estimate, 67 percent of wage costs will be for information generating and handling activities [Vincent, 1984]).

A glut of information which threatens our ability to understand and control business activity.

Growing threats to information integrity, reliability, and privacy as computers and telecommunications distribute information and provide easy access to data.

Information has become the key element in the functioning of our society. Most business transactions are made through credit-based transfers of wealth. (Car rental companies are reluctant to rent for cash: they want a credit card.) Huge industries are set up to handle information or to provide the means for doing so. (Consider IBM and Xerox: if information was unimportant they would disappear.) Government functions and funding are dependent on the availability of large files of personal data about citizens. (Try to do anything related to a governmental activity without a Social Security number and see what happens.) An increasing and significant portion of the world economy is based upon the work of generating, processing, and delivering information.

This is an exciting time. The information age holds promise of better lives for all, but not without risk. John Wicklein says in *The Electronic Nightmare* (1981) that "the tendency in the United States as the 1980s began was to let these developments be decided by the marketplace. No philosophy has been developed on how we should protect ourselves from the unscrupulous use of the new technologies for power or personal enrichment."

Changing Patterns of Information Use

Computers are changing our society and the world. We do not have to understand these effects to use computers; but if we wish to use them carefully and manage our business information resource efficiently we must understand the business implications of the information age.

The computer has brought about changes in our personal lives, in our economy, and in the role of the military. Each of these has important implications for us as managers and individuals. Effects on the individual include the availability of credit, ease of communicating (consider the long distance network), and convenience of travel to distant places. The ready availability of computing power, through local computers and their connections to high-power central computer services, suggests that personal use of computing as both tool and playmate will continue to increase rapidly. The economic effects include mass production at higher quality and lower cost, the emergence of the information and service industries (financial service companies are an example of a new kind of industry based on electronic information), and transferability of skills. The military effects reflect the use of high-technology weapons, shrinking the world and taking away completely the "security" we once felt in having oceans between us and other countries. Computers are a mixed blessing; we have not yet found ways to limit the computer's awesome capabilities to peaceful benefits.

The use of computers is driven inexorably by economics. If the economic cost/benefit curve experienced by the computing industry could be replicated in the automobile industry, a new Chevrolet or Plymouth would cost about $30. Miniaturization and the use of ever more efficient means for conveying signals among and within computer components have meant that the cost per instruction completed has decreased sharply each year, while the speed of completing a process has increased. The most common evidence of this phenomenon is the hand-held calculator. A full-function calculator has dropped in price from about $300 to a $6–$25 range over ten years, while the size has become smaller with each succeeding model.

One aspect of the economics of computing-communications technology is its cost benefits as replacement for human labor. An increasing portion of the labor force is devoted to processing information or providing services. Within service industries as elsewhere, information is becoming a major product (the expensive hospital equipment such as scanners that enhance the ability to do diagnosis are essentially computer-based information generators).

The fastest-growing of elements that make up the overhead or nonproductive portion of the expense of business or government are the administrative costs of handling information. Information handling is the primary task of managers, professionals, and secretaries. With those rapidly increasing costs in mind, one has only to look at the investment per worker (in other words, the capital investment in equipment) to see the problem. Most factory workers represent a per capita investment of around $20,000, while office workers have a per capita investment of only $2000. The computer offers the opportunity to make investments that will attack the costs which are doing the most damage to profits (or in the case of government agencies, budgets). Systems that bring computing power to the personal level—and thereby enhance job productivity and suitability—are most attractive candidates for labor replacement. Improved artifical intelligence and resulting "expert" systems will help managers make decisions from masses of complex data.

Special new applications, including computer-aided design (CAD), computer-aided manufacturing (CAM), and computer-aided engineering (CAE), with robotics as an implementing tool, promise to change most productive work drastically. In a factory, professional designers and engineers are able to approve drawing changes concurrently (CAE), thus making production more efficient. With personal computers we may be able to transfer money among bank accounts, pay bills, and place additional orders for goods and services. In both cases, the user is achieving a faster, more accurate transfer of information.

Miniaturization (with attendant increases in capabilities) is delivering computers that can be embedded in products to make them work better, have more usefulness, and deliver an enhanced flexibility of service. Examples of embedded computers include automobile ignition and fuel systems; automobile dashboard controls; and home appliances such as refrigerators, washing machines, food processors, and television sets. Personal computer users can look forward to a day when all TVs will come with a personal computer built in. Along with the channel fine tuning and color adjustment functions, the computer in your television set of the future will also be a communications controller and "front end" that translates

signals and provides in/out buffer storage to compensate for bit rate differences among devices and communications lines. In some cases, the
television's computer may be a full service personal computer, offering all
the capabilities you have now and using the TV screen as the display,
perhaps with segmented viewing of both television signals and computer
activities. We can anticipate that high-value home appliances will offer
remote diagnostics for service problems. A remote service center, connected to your washing machine or stereo, could tell you what is wrong
and give instructions on your purchase and installation of the appropriate
parts. Your bank could transmit account data to your TV computer's data
store each night (say, between midnight and 6:00 A.M.). Then whenever
you wanted to see the status of your account, you would have only to push
a button or two. Your job as executive or manager can be made more
efficient by your being able to move information around directly from home
or office. All or many of these computer uses have important communications elements: an essential part of our story in this book. Computers
almost always end up meaning *communication* of information. And information is valuable.

From the smoke signal to the semaphore, then the telegraph, the telephone, the radio, and finally the computer we can trace a continued development of communications technology as humans have tried to move
information ever faster and more efficiently. The telephone is part of the
industrial age, but the computer has made the telephone network—essentially a grid of copper wires—an information-age tool. This leap forward
occurred when automatic long distance dialing became possible in the 1960s
with the development at Bell Laboratories of the first automatic telephone
switch, the #1–ESS. Today, telephone switching centers are banks of computers; their reliability and flexibility in selecting "best routing" has resulted in a fantastic worldwide communications capability. Remember that
in 1946, in the United States, almost all long distance calls required going
through a series of operators and that in 1956 in European suburban areas,
many telephone systems required operator assistance on every call.

In the 1960s, the computers embedded in the telephone allowed users
to connect with distant computers with a lot of power, computers they
could never have afforded individually. Today, our personal computers
provide several times the power these early time-sharing users had, but
communication still offers the key to enjoying the really beneficial services
from computing, providing us with cheap access to large central computers.

Computer systems designers provide security elements that *logically* separate their particular system or network from all others. But all systems
or computers connected to a network, including the ubiquitous telephone
system, are *physically* interconnected with all other networks. This will
always be true, because a network connection at any point will eventually
lead to a communications switch. Since we can never afford to replace all

the investments in communications facilities, we are led through the communications switch into the grid of wires, radio links, and submarine cables that connects all the parts of the world. The separation of the many systems and networks is a logical separation, caused by differing protocols, software, hardware barriers, and operating procedures. However, the fact of physical connection means that knowledgeable people can often overcome or bypass these barriers and by finding clever routings can go from one system to another.

Many of my friends work for other high-tech companies. Although our business networks are logically separate (Xerox networks do not interconnect with the networks of other companies), we have almost always been able to find a way to communicate via our personal computers. We find a network (for example, ARPANET, the government-sponsored research net) with which both our networks connect. We then use that network as an interconnect link. Logically, we are not connected; physically, we know we are connected because of the communications switches and the communications grid that are the backbone for all telecommunications. (Figure 2.1 on page 19 illustrates this common physical network.) This obviously has security and privacy implications for business, government, and private computer users.

The Great Computer Crime Scare

> Working solely from the base of sensational news stories concerning "Computer Crime" is certain to distort and perhaps cripple efforts at rational control of losses. (Eason and Webb, 1983; p. 19)

Many people dislike watching the television news because it depresses them. A truism in television news and the press is the fact that readers are not interested in good news, something that is demonstrated by the success of sensational journalism. To attract readers, the press apparently must offer ever more sensational headlines. One recent favorite for getting reader interest and attention is the reporting of so-called computer crime.

Sellers of security systems and hardware have taken up the story. Security consultants are understandably fond of tales that strike terror into the hearts of business managers: embarrassing publicity, loss of resources, and lawsuits resulting from fraudulent use of computers or external penetration into business computer systems. Without doubt, there is a danger; there have been many cases of computer-related fraud and damages resulting from unauthorized access to business computer files.

Let us consider a few press reports drawn from many over the recent past, and examine them with logic.

Data Business (United Kingdom), April 1982, in a report by Jay Thompson, "Milking the Machines, Drop by Stealthy Drop," says that we should forget the spectacular frauds and worry about the "fiddles"—the small cases where employees who use computer systems are able to modify or bypass procedure and take out goods or cash. These are frauds in the $10,000–to-$50,000 range.... The author correctly addresses the most severe risk, failed or poor procedural controls.

Computerweek (South Africa), January 1982, reports in an article by Leonard Fine, "Computer Crime—Myth or Reality?," that rapidly changing technology, highly skilled personnel, changing social values, and a fast-moving external environment contribute to an escalating risk exposure.... What Fine says here is true, but actual experience has been that most computer-related crimes are committed by clerical and managerial people, very few by technical experts.

EDPACS newsletter (Automation Training Center, Reston, Va.), July 1982, reported a case involving the J. Walter Thompson advertising agency. The agency had to write off $30 million in earnings because data were fraudulently entered into the firm's computer by a vice president. The firm's chairman said "In today's world, you are ever more dependent on the personal integrity of people."... The comment fails to address the missing or inadequate procedural controls that allowed such entry of un-validated income.

Any informed citizen must be concerned about misuse of computers, but business managers are especially concerned. They are concerned about loss of resources, of course, but probably even more by the specter of lawsuits by shareholders or customers. However, a practical view should prevail, one that sees the problem in the broader terms of information management rather than specifically as security vulnerability.

There are two problems with the view reflected in popular-press reports of spectacular "computer crimes." First, there is no widely accepted definition, so anyone can compile and publish extremely misleading statistics; these reports are also frequently based on incorrectly or carelessly assembled data. Second, there is no established requirement (except in the banking industry) for reporting computer-related crimes, so one reads in the press about only very large, impossible-to-hide frauds, thus skewing attention toward the high-value cases.

A Definition

If a reasonable definition is in operation even some of the more spectacular cases become suspect and many others must be rejected. Let us therefore propose a working definition:

Computer crime is a crime in which the use of or access to a computer or its component parts (terminals, networks, and so on) is an essential element; that is, the crime could not have been committed without the use of a computer.

This definition meets the rational goals for identifying a class of crime, which should be (1) to allow protective measures to be designed to prevent repetition and (2) to allow prosecution of those involved against an established statute with set penalities, thus further discouraging such crimes. Frequent confusion of the use of the computer as an *essential* with its use as an *incidental* compromises a rational approach. Consider the variety of possible misuse of computers and computer-related electronic information resources, which might include:

Fraud and embezzlement

Theft of computing services

Mischief (the "hackers")

Theft of information

Attacks on (nonphysical) computer resources

Based on experience, these appear in order of frequency; fraud and embezzlement are by far the most widespread types of computer misuse. However, consider the 1983 U.S. Department of Justice Report on Crimes Involving Electronic Funds Transfer (EFT), which noted the following conclusions:

The actual level of corporate crime involving computers is probably small [sic].

EFT crime is only a small portion of all financial crimes.

Crime using automated teller machines is no worse than it would be using paper-based systems.

Consumer fraud could be *reduced* using EFT systems.

So the most frequently reported type of crime using computers is seen as a "minor" category. Theft-of-services cases, probably the second most frequent, usually amount to less than $100,000 in value. The widely publicized numbers are taken out of context and often involve a distortion of facts. Recently a case involving the theft of a truckload of microcomputers was widely hailed as a "multimillion-dollar computer crime." Our definition of a computer-related crime deflates this claim and others like it.

In a famous case (Equity Fund) involving the creation of fictitious assets by management, we must question it being reported as a computer-related crime. Although the culprits used computers to fabricate insurance policies, it is conceivable that in past times a similar document forgery could have occurred using manual means and a copier. In contrast, a case where a bank official kited loans to allow himself enormous personal credits involved the computer as an essential, because the perpetrator used a weakness in the computer processing controls to cover his fraud; he processed a stream of documents to cover illegitimate loans. A case reported in several national magazines was the theft of illicit funds transfer, of several million dollars. While labeled a computer crime, the theft was made possible when the perpetrator observed a code word carelessly left unprotected. He then made a telephone call ordering the transfer and authorizing it by use of the code word. At this point no computers had been used. The bank then transferred the money as directed, using a computer. But the fraud was committed without a computer—and the transfer could have been made by telegram.

The computer-security industry has no corner on the use of hyperbole for scarce purposes. A commonly reported statistic for a number of years has been that 43 percent of all businesses having a computer-room fire failed within three years. This statistic was eventually traced to a 1949 article in the *Journal of Commerce* stating that 43 percent of companies without adequate business insurance failed after serious fires (*Computer Security Newsletter* [January–February 1983], p. 1). There were no business computers in use in 1949.

In addition to the distortions caused by careless definition, reported data have suffered serious inflation. Just recently at a conference of security people, a speaker cited statistics indicating that while the average bank robbery was worth $1500, the average computer crime had a value of over $350,000. When challenged, the speaker said the data were "from the FBI." A survey by the American Institute of Certified Public Accountants (*Data Communications* [May 1983]) tells a much different story. Sixty-four percent of computer-related crimes were of values less than $9000; only 7.1 percent were worth more than $250,000 (Naisbitt, 1982). These data put the matter more truly in perspective. Although incident values of bank robberies and computer crimes may be roughly equal, there are many more bank robberies each year (tens of thousands in the United States) and most robberies carry the risk of physical harm.

Practical business managers must conclude that, at least for the near future, computer-related crime is a matter for concern, but there is no epidemic and large numbers of businesses are not going bankrupt as a result. Precipitate action is neither appropriate nor prudent. The risk is not from computers; the risk is a larger one of threats to business information in general.

The business manager who recognizes the importance of the information resource needs to have a balanced view of the computer-related crime threat, and several important points must be considered in arriving at a considered position:

1. Computers are essential to the operation of business and the workings of society in the information age; properly applied, computers offer benefits greater than any other tool. We could then say that some acceptance of risk is worthwhile.
2. Information stored in or processed on computers can be provided security safeguards equivalent to or better than those afforded information in other forms. In other words, computer systems have the potential for extremely rigorous, highly resistant security measures that meet or exceed the best security available for other business assets. The required level of security for highly valued business information in electronic forms may be expensive, but it can be provided with currently available technology.
3. Actual cases involving information theft, disclosure, or damage most often involve printed data. In second place must be data in mental form distributed through careless talk, rumor, or intentional disclosure. Fraud, theft, or misuse involving electronic forms probably takes third place. While there have been a number of cases reported as computer crimes involving computer-generated data, in most instances the data were transferred in printed form.

The key question then may be "How did the parties to the crime most often attack?" In most cases for which reliable information is available, the crime developed because of the availability of information *on paper*. Certainly the miscreants could have generated the paper through illicit use of a business computer; however, to date the facts have been otherwise in the vast majority of cases. In the IBM/Hitachi industrial espionage case (1983), the information was all on paper when transferred.

At a major data center of a large American company, all briefcases are searched for magnetic tapes. Rather large documents could presumably be carried through without question. It follows that anyone wishing to abscond with valuable information would print it out, then remove it from the premises. Of course, if the data were already in printed form, one would only need access to a copier. If briefcases were also being searched for reports, the stolen documents (or floppy disks) could easily have been sent out of the data center via company or public mails, which are not searched.

The astute business manager, then, must make careful judgments. All forms of valued business information must be protected in a consistent and effective manner, within prudent risk-management practice. Absolute security is never possible for any business resource; since business itself is a process of taking measured risk, that should not bother us. A much broader and more appropriate issue for concern is the management of the business information resource. Security is an important subset of that matter.

2 | The Manager's Perspective on Threats to Business Information

> *As methods of manufacturing and commerce have evolved, methods of criminal attacks on such operations have also become more sophisticated. Most recently computers have become a tool for businessmen. They assist in record keeping of all kinds and in developing his general business strategies at all levels . . . unfortunately, computers also further remove the businessman from day-to-day supervision.*
>
> *—S. W. Liebholz and L. D. Wilson (1974, p. ix)*

Scare stories and hyperbole concerning so-called computer crime should be taken on balance, but there *are* serious threats to business information with which the business manager must be concerned. These threats—perhaps better called vulnerabilities—result from developing societal, personal, and business trends. The proliferation and importance of electronic information forms is one of these trends, but others must also be understood if a practical and effective information protection program is to be developed. Always remember that protection is only a part of an overall information resource management effort.

Managers must consider the potential for attacks both on the information resource and on the information-processing and storage infrastructure. The latter consists of the physical assets: computers, storage media (tape libraries, disks, and the like), and telecommunications systems used in the business operations. Protection for the physical infrastructure is a matter of physical security controls and protection measures, a concern similar to that for manufacturing or distribution facilities. In the past the information infrastructure was the more critical concern because of its cost and relative scarcity. Today that is no longer the case; computing hardware is cheaper and replacement no longer requires extensive lead times. Proper contingency planning nevertheless remains essential (see Chapter 10).

In the information age, then, it is the information content and not the systems infrastructure that must be of primary concern to management. The information itself is the valuable: information may be irreplaceable; its value may exceed that of all other resources; and its misuse may result in fraud or loss of competitive edge.

General Information Vulnerabilities

Foremost among present serious threats to business information resources are lack of motivation and decline in pride of workmanship (and thus loyalty) among employees. The resulting careless errors are generally regarded as the primary threat to information integrity. (Errors are not a security matter but a general supervisory management concern having to do with systems design, training, motivation, and control.) The business information resource manager must address current and potential error problems through good systems design, effective employee training, strong supervision, and efficient controls throughout the business process. It is especially important to ensure that controls continue to be workable and effective when manual systems are converted to computer processing and wherever information changes form (as in data entry operations).

The Paper Chase

The primary risk to business information today is its theft or misuse in written form by employees. Paper is easy to carry around—and out. Most critical business information regarding strategy, results of research, new product plans, and so forth exists in written forms. The widespread use of copiers makes protecting this information extremely difficult. Management's key task, at least during the next decade, will be to establish and maintain employee loyalty and to set policies and procedures that will identify, value, and control written information.

A second information vulnerabilty is the malfeasance of trusted employees authorized access to electronic forms of business information, in some cases the very people who developed the information. A survey several years ago of computer programmers indicated that a majority considered programs written on company time to be their own property. The lack of respect for the property of others evidenced by the casual theft and destruction of our cities' equipment and facilities carries over into the business workplace. Many employees deny the employer rights as owner of intangibles; the information resource manager must establish the means to defend those rights—in court, if necessary. This includes using proprietary information protection agreements and other employment contract stipulations to establish a legal right at the time of employment. Policies setting forth practices regarding management and use of the business information resource and associated computing equipment should be enforced. Both are important should legal remedies be necessary.

Last in order of risk to information is the outsider, the industrial espionage agent or casual penetrator who purposefully attempts to penetrate privacy and security barriers to obtain, change, or destroy information illicitly. This type of threat is much less common than the first two. A professional agent is almost impossible to protect against. He or she may be well trained and an employee of long standing at the time the damage is done. A well-thought-out, carefully designed information resource protection program is the best defense and one that will provide legal recourse should protection fail. Many times outsiders gain access to business information through veteran or recently hired employees. These people are usually not professional agents, but simply opportunistic individuals who will seize every chance for enrichment. The information involved is usually in written form, on pieces of paper, when the information theft occurs.

Information in electronic form, in process or transmission or on magnetic media, may be an element in any of the vulnerabilities described above. This is an important point. The electronic form of information may lend itself to certain attacks on business information, but it must be regarded as only one vulnerability among several so that all forms of information are adequately protected.

The variety of ways in which an intelligent person can attack business information in electronic forms appears endless: a recent article in *Computing*, the British computing newspaper described some unusually innovative Italian computer-abuse schemes (January 22, 1984; p. 34). Every defensive system devised is immediately countered with a new method of attack; a "complete list" of the vulnerabilties of computer information must always be suspect, because the fertile brains of computer experts can always come up with a new attack, one for which no defense has yet been invented. But the more common methods are as follows:

1. Hands-on attacks. These may be made by managers, clerks, computer operators, or bank tellers, among others. Usually these attacks are by people who have authorized use of some input or processing stage of a system. Through understanding of the details of system operation or controls, these employees (or outsiders) can attempt fraudulent transactions or may be able to cover such actions by clever manipulation of the system. An example would be the entering of false merchandise returns data or the practice of kiting, substituting other people's deposits to cover improper withdrawals. Such actions usually require collusion on the part of others, often people in other businesses with which transactions are performed.
2. Communications access using "hard wired" or dial-up remote-access facilities to obtain information or to interfere with the intended processes in the central computer. Intruders may find that a telephone call will connect with a central computer; through clever testing the sign-on process and password are derived and the attacker is able to perform the functions of an authorized user. Poor password construction and

weak security discipline among a population of users can make such connections easy. The intruder can browse through files or cause mischief. Such penetrations are fairly common in widely shared systems, and include the "hacker" attacks often reported by the press.

3. Communications network penetrations, including wiretapping and radio interceptions. The attacker may be able to record data traffic for later analysis, add spurious data (for example, to effect a transfer of funds), or replace sections of traffic. Connection with or interception of communications is surprisingly simple if the technology is understood.

4. Software-based attack using the operating system facilities intended for maintenance. The attacker may be able to modify software programs to cause certain instructions to bypass security controls or to introduce a program that will react to a certain stimulus (such as a date or a set of data) to move files or perform processes contrary to the intent of the system designer. Often, these things are possible because of ever-present errors or omissions in the operating system programs. Terms such as *logic bombs*, *Trojan horses*, and the like refer to software-based attacks. The most likely perpetrator of such an attack would be an employee with authorized use of privileged code. But software attacks from outside are also possible and have occurred in publicized cases in which the attacker gained access via a terminal and network and clandestinely made changes to system controls.

This sample of risk types suggests that certain circumstances are especially vulnerable. In order of diminishing risk, today's electronic information vulnerabilities are:

1. Communication or distribution of information through networks or dial-up telephone connections. There are two aspects to this vulnerability. First, there is no currently affordable positive method for identifying the person or program attempting to make a connection and displaying authorization to do so. Work on better means for identification and authentication is under way, but usual current methods are woefully inadequate if really vulnerable information is involved. Second, the transmission systems are not equipped with robust security elements. Opportunities for illicit connection with or penetration of information networks are usually plentiful. These may occur because of weaknesses in the physical and electronic components and their surrounding environment or as a result of software errors. (One of the things we can always rely on in the field of electronic information is that there *will* be errors in software, including some in the programs we rely upon to guarantee security.)

2. Distribution of business information files and elements to local, personal processors, and to special-purpose data bases in office computers, exposing the information resource to improper use. Data stored on disks

in a data center can be fairly well protected and access and use controlled by the information resource manager. Once delivered to a local computer or personal workstation, proper use and protection must depend on the person having possession. A number of special risks occur in these situations. The information may be processed against unauthorized or faulted software, thus generating summary data that could be misleading or useful for fraudulent purposes. Electronic forms can readily be converted to written or mental form and carried away for sale to competitors without the inconvenience of having to bypass security systems that may constrain such activity in data centers or central offices. Such security systems (usually physical in form) may be virtually useless if general employee loyalties are suspect.

Once in electronic form in a distributed processing system or network, information is like water in plumbing. It is ready for use at the turn of a faucet—or a computer switch. In such circumstances traditional procedures for monitoring and controlling written information become worthless.

High-Tech Risks

An important point in our consideration of electronic information vulnerabilities is the high-tech environment in which many employees now work.

Pressures for success and its trappings in a materialistic culture may lead employees to an "anything goes, what's in it for me?" philosophy. The profile of some individuals caught in computer-related crime is that of highly educated achievers with no criminal background. Since the use of computers—especially by the extremely capable, involved person—results in significant power over business controls and resources, failure to accept individual responsibility can create problems. Purposeful, *authorized* use of computing may show clever people how to do innovative, unusual, *unauthorized* things. Increasing skills and perhaps a chance discovery may uncover opportunity for fun and eventual profit. Fortunately, most people are honest, but computers may deliver temptations which eventually prove irresistible. Employee screening will not identify all potential computer criminals; they are the very people most businesses would want to hire. Ethics, unfortunately, is seldom a part of computer training.

Employee motivation, training, and awareness are critical if business information resources are to be controlled in the electronic age. Security technology is a help; but without the interest and concern of the majority of employees, trouble will eventually occur. The serious threats about which managers must be concerned have to do with mundane things like procedures, training, motivation, and supervision.

Personal Computing: Cause for Concern

If you use a personal computer, at work or at home or in both places, you are among the technological leaders in the decade of the eighties. But you will not be a member of the elite for long. By 1990 most Americans will have personal computers, probably run in tandem with their home television sets, and many of these computers will be connected with information networks. The computer is the tool that has created the economic and technological forces which brought this new information age. The personal computer has far-reaching implications for information control in both business and personal life. Stewart Brand, writing in his *Whole Earth Software Catalog* (1984), says that the arrival of personal computing has caused a shift in power between individuals and institutions. We will discuss this important business tool at length to understand its impact.

With personal computers people will be enjoying the benefits of information technology at the personal level and there are many joys. But there are also drawbacks. The proliferation and replication and communication of trillions of pieces of information can cause serious trouble. Figure 2.1 illustrates some of the security vulnerabilities of the personal computer and its potential connections.

One illustration of the negative side of the information age is the volume of information on file in governmental agencies concerning individuals and businesses. The military, intelligence agencies, Social Security, motor vehicle, and welfare files contain the equivalent of the dossiers maintained by military dictatorships. The use of personal computers and telecommunications for credit and message purposes will expand this central electronic collection of information. Most people already believe that the government and the public utilities are gathering and sharing personal information based on telephone conversations and credit-related activity (*The New York Times* "Privacy Threats Worry Americans" December 8, 1983).

The Personal Computer: Glamour Product of the 1980s

Probably no other product has ever received the sensational coverage, the excited discussion, or the outright hype that attended the marketing of the personal computer. The development of products and services in the personal computing area has been phenomenal both in numbers and in profits. IBM Corporation is expected to have gross annual sales of $4 billion in personal computers; that, by itself as a product line, is bigger than most major corporations' gross. The personal computer is sold using one or more sales approaches:

> People need personal computers to have a complete education (a tack especially strong with families with school children).

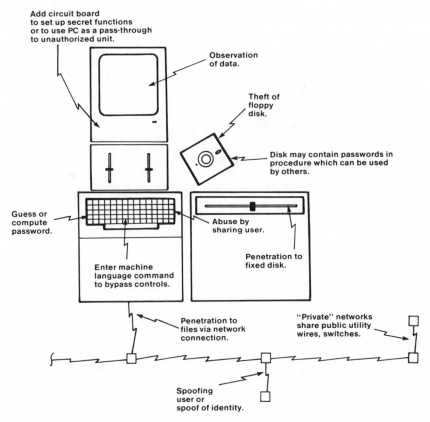

Figure 2.1 Potential vulnerabilities of the personal computer.

People find computers useful in maintaining control of their personal environment (bank accounts, investments, shopping, home budgets, and heat, light, air conditioning).

One needs a personal computer for the fun of playing games and thus improvement of electronic skills (learning to relate to computers).

Business people need the computer to help with work from their jobs or business.

Probably only the last two reasons are even partially valid; very few people are going to have jobs using computers in relation to the overall working population. And the difficulties in establishing and maintaining home records and controls with a computer are far greater than the work involved in doing things the old manual way. Finally, a few people will need to understand the workings of computers. But for the masses, including business managers and educators, understanding the details of computer programming will be the equivalent of understanding the workings of automobile engines. It's nice to know, but certainly not an essential.

Anyone who already has a computer and is an "average" person is probably using the software provided (or bought separately) to do various things he or she enjoys or finds helpful. Most personal computer users will therefore not write programs for the tasks they wish to accomplish. Writing software is an art that takes a special capability, a lot of study, or both. Most personal computer users will choose to buy proven software packages rather than struggle with the tedium of writing and testing programs. Too, most personal computer users "trust" the software they purchase; they assume that the software will do what it claims to do, and nothing more or less. This trust is a vulnerability that could make users susceptible to a loss of security or invasion of privacy, a subject we will return to later.

Finally, users will sooner or later succumb to the temptation to connect with some kind of communications services for their personal computers. One very appealing part of the personal computing phenomenon is the services available through telecommunications, such as message systems, banking, information services (Teletext, for example), and buying. We can see this glamorous product interfaced with the home television electronics configuration, operated by purchased software, connected with outside network services, and used for business and pleasure.

Services from Personal Computing

A wide array of services is available from the packaged software and hardware delivered with the purchase of a microcomputer system. This impressive set of services is further expandable if the user is willing to write programs to expand or add to the packaged software, or to spend the money to buy more hardware. In the future, computing "utilities" will offer connected microcomputer users even more service options; the utility will charge a fee, similar to a telephone service fee, that will allow connection with a network offering catalog shopping, banking, information retrieval services, and so forth. This provision of services to the home and business microcomputer user will become a major industry; it is now in its infancy with such network services as Source.

For the sake of discussion, we can place all microcomputing services into three arbitrary classifications:

Information storage and retrieval (IS&R)

Processing or computing

Telecommunications

Each of these kinds of services has particular security and privacy considerations that we will address. Most times the microcomputer user will be applying combinations of these service classifications to meet a particular need.

Information Storage and Retrieval

This category of microcomputer service can be thought of as a replacement for paper. We use information storage and retrieval (IS&R) to record information, to store it in a secure place and in a form which allows us to retrieve it efficiently, and then to recall the data as needed. Think about writing a note to yourself to remember to buy your mother-in-law a birthday gift. Three actions are involved: first you write the note; then you put it someplace you will be able to see it or retrieve it; finally, you see it and buy the gift at the appropriate time. Computers provide an ideal medium for such activities. They provide efficient ways to record data; they encourage us to be orderly and to use tools like file names and indexes when information is stored. When we are ready to retrieve the information, the computer can display an index and provide various pieces of identifying data about the files.

These are very simple examples. In many business systems, vast amounts of data are stored in specialized file structures (data bases) designed to make the access and retrieval and further processing of information more efficient. Microcomputer users have database software available to them in the many packages offered for the purpose.

Processing

Computers were originally developed to do processing, that is, to perform arithmetic functions many times faster than any other method or machine. Included in such processing are functions such as comparing or matching. Using logic gates, which provide "and/or" capabilities, computers can sort digital forms of information. Sorting of information elements is a very common form of data processing. The mathematical work (calculating or "computing") performed by scientists, engineers, and financial analysts is "pure" processing.

Most microcomputer functions are combinations of IS&R and data processing. Word processing, mostly information storage and retrieval, uses very little of the computer's data processing capabilities. Mathematical work, on the other hand, uses mostly information-processing capabilities and very little IS&R. Data processing or "number-crunching" is the heart of computing. Although microcomputer users may not typically use the data-processing power of their computers to a great degree, it is the critical function and provides the basis for all other services.

Telecommunications

Communications are the essence of the information age. Computers imbedded in telephone networks allow us the luxury of direct-dial connections to virtually anyplace in the world. Computer-to-computer communications are convenient as a result of computer switches and computer conversion units that can translate various modes and formats. Telecommunications offers the microcomputer user the capability to contact or access information sources anywhere in the world. Obviously, telecommunications also constitutes the greatest vulnerability in terms of information privacy and security. Once our information is outside the confines of our home or business, we lose control. And while our computer system is connected to any network, we must be concerned about outsiders penetrating our system and on-line files.

Personal Computer Configurations

Because there are so many manufacturers of personal computers and of peripheral attachments, we have an almost limitless variety of configurations available. When the various hardware elements are considered along with the wide range of software packages now on the market, the potential buyer of a microcomputer system is faced with a bewildering array of options. The situation is made even more complex by the relative lack of reliability and candor in marketing these products. Computer systems professionals often do not have personal computers at home, mostly because they refuse to believe the claims of those selling these products. These professionals know that a relatively inexpensive personal computer often creates more problems than it solves; they also know that all software has shortcomings that can cause a lot of misery for the user. Most important, of course, they realize that there are few practical home applications. These reservations, which should give any buyer pause, also have important privacy and security implications for the user who will rely on the microcomputer for financial or other confidential applications.

The microcomputer may be considered in terms of four general configurations:

1. Minimal stand-alone, where a processor, keyboard, display, small disk or tape store, and elementary printer are used for personal applications using purchased or self-developed software. In many cases, only keyboard, processor, and display are found and the unit is used primarily for games and other entertainment-related applications.
2. Dial-up network connected, where the configuration in number 1 has access to a public utility network via a modem and telephone line. Through the network, this configuration has access to other computers and services such as message systems.

3. Time-sharing, where a minimal configuration, perhaps only processor and keyboard, has dial-up or direct access to a cental computer. Processing, printing, and other services may be done centrally. In this case the microcomputer acts as a terminal; of course, local processing may also be done. Data stores might be central or local.

4. Local area network server, where the microcomputer is one of a series connected to a very high speed local area network (LAN). There may be a local printer or disk store; there will be central printing, storage, and communications services. The LAN may or may not be connected with outside public utility networks or with other LANs. This configuration is the most advanced and highest-capability form of microcomputing. Because of the cost, this configuration is usually found only in businesses, universities, or government agencies.

Microcomputer Applications

The microcomputer, especially in an extended configuration, offers the user flexibility and power that allow the choice of many interesting and helpful applications. These applications may be considered as being in six general classes:

1. Games and entertainment, many times in conjunction with home television equipment. All home television will eventually be microcomputer-equipped.

2. Accounting and financial, with features assisting the user in specialized activities, such as stock portfolio or general investment management. This is the most common form of application.

3. Communications services, including shopping, message systems, banking transactions, information services (videotext), bulletin boards, and so forth, using applications with software and source data at other locations remote to the user.

4. Home services, such as environmental (HVAC) control, appliance timing and control, security, lighting, and child observation. Menu planning and shopping-list assembly are other applications in this class, although it is difficult to imagine practical use for these in most households.

5. Word processing, an important common application for a majority of early personal computer users. The powerful word processing software and high-quality printers available today make composition and assembly of documents highly efficient.

6. Education, where keyboard and display provide tools for teaching and learning. Educational packages are probably much more important than the computer-use skills obtained through general microcomputer operation; educational packages could lead to development of a major industry in the near future.

Each application has different security implications. The microcomputer user should be aware of the vulnerabilities of each application so that proper safeguards may be taken. See Chapter 4 for more detailed discussion of personal computer security.

3 | The Information Resource

Information, which in essence is the analysis and synthesis of data, will unquestionably be one of the most vital of corporate resources in the 1980's. It will be structured in models for planning and decision making. It will be incorporated into measurements of performance and profitability. In other words, information will be recognized and treated as an asset.

—John Diebold (1979)

The security concerns naturally developed by reports of computer-related crime must be addressed in the context of the overall business environment. Our concern, therefore, is less with computer crime itself than with the management issue of controlling the information resource. Security is properly seen as an element of information resource management. To do otherwise avoids facing the real issue and is "not seeing the forest for the trees."

The relative importance of business resources—people, raw materials, financial assets, plant and equipment, and information—is changing. Information has become the critical business resource, the single element that can make the difference between business success and failure. Employees who are skilled, courageous, and hard-working continue to be essential to business success; substitutes for most other resources can be found or discovered. But information is most critical because it provides competence, generated by experience, analysis, and planning.

Business managers have long recognized the need to manage and protect important resources. Generally, the more important the resource to the business and/or the more immediate value a resource has, the greater the management effort expended. A new product design is shielded in the laboratory so that the casual passer-by cannot see it; cash is locked in vaults and carefully counted each day. These highly valued business resources are tangibles with physical attributes and pose no unusual problem concerning management measures for conservation.

Information, being intangible, requires fresh management thinking and new protection methods. For example, innovative insurance policies covering information resources are becoming available. Managers must rethink their old ideas about business security as economics and competitive pressures drive business to seek out and apply technology information. The most successful businesses will be those which devote a significant portion of their financial strength to research, seeking ever more efficient methods and applications of technology, resulting in an increasingly valuable information base. Information means not only better products and the promise of increasing sales but also reduced costs through efficiency of production.

In the United States we have many examples of businesses that failed to recognize the importance of technology. On the other hand, Chrysler Corporation's revitalization resulted in most part from production automation and other applications of technology. Chrysler had to seek out information on how to improve production efficiency and lower costs, information on how to engineer and build front-wheel-drive automobiles, information on automation, information on innovative corporate financing, and information on the marketplace and what consumers wanted in modern cars. Much of this information concerned or was developed through applications of technology. Certainly, in its struggle to renew, Chrysler had to be concerned about the management and protection of this information, which was developed as a critical competitive resource.

This suggests that information important to business operation is being extended beyond the traditional business files to include strategic and technical information. Customer lists, prospect lists, accounts receivable, inventories, and other routine business information take on added importance as competition becomes ever more intense. At the same time, the widespread use and new applications of computers tied in networks have increased business vulnerabilities to information misuse.

A crucial new element has therefore appeared for business and industry: the information resource of competitive technology. For only a few businesses is technology not important, and to disregard technology today is to risk being overtaken in the race for business and profits. A competitor with unique information—gained in any manner—may have the winning edge. Information may represent important business technology investments in several forms, including:

1. Information generated by research activities, which may not be immediately or directly related to product or operational requirements but may form the basis for a future coup.
2. Information concerning business operations methods, computer processes, production techniques, market strategies, and other applications giving potential business advantage.
3. Information about specific processes or controls, such as the computer programs that direct a robot, computer-assisted design or manufacturing software, and market analysis software.

4. Information concerning ongoing business decisions and the background for those decisions, including information concerning a competitor's technology and decisions based on that information.

Any given element of business information may have significant value. Decisions about that value and the appropriate management measures are an important issue addressed later in this book (see Chapter 4). Technology and its information forms, however, and the impact and import of those competitive technology information elements, are the crux of the business manager's information management concern.

Information merits increased management attention. Information is an essential that must be categorized, managed with skill, conserved, and protected. Senior business managers must recognize the value of information to the business and take actions to direct its management and control. Subordinate information managers and security managers must provide effective means for valuing, organizing, and protecting the information resource.

Types and Forms of Information

Several types and forms of information can be identified. Although not directly essential to protecting information, acknowledging the types and forms enables the manager to make better decisions concerning information *valuation*. Valuation is an important step in the process of information management and is critical to defining security needs. (In Chapter 4 we shall see how identifying types and forms of information aids in setting information values and, in the end, determining management actions required to conserve the information resource.)

For our purposes, business information can be said to occur as three *types*:

1. Developmental information (projections concerning markets, products, financial management, and business strategies) and the outputs of research activities (which may include pure research concepts; technology applications; and research laboratory notebooks, results, and proposals).
2. Dynamic information, which includes all the data generated in the course of managing ongoing current operations. Information in this category includes such data as production output levels, quality control monitoring data, current sales, current receivables, stock levels, raw material levels, in-process engineering changes, pricing and price adjustments, and unannounced pending organizational changes.
3. Historical information, which includes such records of past business operations as payables, proprietorship data, business results (profit and loss), personnel records, records kept to meet the requirements of law, and computer-system recovery files.

This is not a complete list, of course, nor is the placement of items in the lists other than illustrative. Many accountants will argue that receivables is a historical information type. The precise assignment of records to types is not important at this point. When it becomes important the decision will be more evident in light of the decision-maker's knowledge of the business and its characteristics.

The *forms* of information are both relevant and important to decisions about information management and security. The form of an information element directly relates to its perception by the user or its substantial quality. Thus the forms as we will consider them are mental, written, and electronic.

Mental information is that carried in the human brain. Tradition is an example of mental information of the historical type. In past ages, mental information was the only source of intelligence on how to do things; it remains an important data source and is a useful storehouse of valuable business data. Consider how often a business will pay a premium to attract and employ a manager who has certain skills based on mental information. Businesses wishing to manage the information resource must consider the mentally stored information carried about by employees. Obviously, reasonable control is a matter of employee motivation and loyalty; businesses can nevertheless take steps to establish legal barriers to improper use of mental information, usually in the form of employment contracts or non-disclosure agreements.

Written information encompasses all the books, documents, and papers used throughout the business world. The greatest store of information is in written form, although electronic form is making significant inroads. It is said that more books are written each year, in the information age, than were written in all recorded history before 1950. Written information does not lend itself to efficient retrieval. Anyone who has researched a term paper, report, or book knows that locating precise information is tedious and time-consuming. Also, because paper is not a permanent medium, information stored in written form can deteriorate.

Electronic information is becoming the standard for time-sensitive business data. It is remarkably free of the time and space constraints associated with information in written form. Mental information has limitations of recall and portability that render it suspect in comparison to electronic forms. Within a few years, all information except private mental information will at one point in its life cycle occur in electronic form. Typesetting in publishing today uses computers, although the final storage medium is still paper. The cost of electronic storage is decreasing so significantly that it will soon be cheaper to store and retrieve information from a library of books on laser disks than to use traditional library methods. Before ad-

Table 3.1 Information Forms and Characteristics

System info form	Storage	Retrieval	Transfer	Density	Process
Written	Inconvenient	Slow	Slow	Low	Inefficient
Electronic	Fast	Fast	Fast	High	Efficient
Mental	Fast but inefficient	Fast but unreliable	Slow	Very high	Efficient but limited

dressing the management of the information resource, consider Table 3.1, which illustrates the forms of information and some of the intersecting characteristics from a manager's view.

Information Management

Management consultant John Diebold has suggested that a key management responsibility for the 1980s is Information Resource Management, or IRM. But while there is a present wealth of references on how to manage other business resources such as people, plant, inventories, and cash, not much is commonly known about managing the resource called information. Many managers simply assume they know how to do it because it is a self-evident process. Unfortunately for them, in the age of information there is much to be learned, especially when computers are used as the primary means for developing, distributing, analyzing, and publishing business information. Once the manager recognizes the types and forms of information and acknowledges its value to the business, the requirements for its management become clearer.

We would not expect a manager to treat all inventories (iron ore, pencils, railroad cars, gasoline) the same but rather to devise some specialized handling for each according to its category and place in the business scheme. To do a good job of managing information managers must think through how this vital resource occurs, what it costs, how it is applied, and what rational management decisions are called for. A comparison of information resource control responsibilities with those for other business resources is provided in Table 3.2.

We will examine several aspects of information management: costs, organization for business use, "ownership" concepts, data management, and records management.

Business Information Costs

Most business managers instinctively realize that information is not free, but they have acted as though it were. As the world moves into the information age, the cost of the information resource used in business will

Table 3.2 Comparative Business Resource Management Actions

Resources	Activity valuation	Control	Security	General management
Materials	Replacement or actual cost	Inventory counts, Issue controls	Physical protection methods	Materials management, Procurement, Inventory
Information	Damages from loss, exposure or inaccuracy	Authorization for use	Logical and procedural controls	Information management, Systems controls
Financial resources	Actual or discounted	Bookkeeping Counts of cash	Procedures, methods, vaults	Investment, business uses, Financial analysis

become an ever-increasing proportion of the total business operating cost. For some companies, a very significant part of wages costs will be expended for information handling, ranging upwards to 90% of payroll. Paul Strassmann of Xerox has estimated that real information costs in a business amount to about 88 times the annual data-processing investment. Further, information may pose a potential cost in terms of liability, should actual or purported damages to customers or society be demonstrated from management lack of due care (especially in the use of computers).

Information Organization for Business Use

Information organization may be considered objective or subjective, groupings that are useful for assigning values and determining records management strategies. Usually, both objective and subjective considerations are in play. *Objective organization* of information refers to arrangement of information according to its use in the business. Accounts receivable data are likely to be organized in a way that facilitates its major purpose, the collection of monies due. Hence, accounts receivable are usually organized by customer. The data structures established for control and retrieval of information in computer data bases are examples of information skillfully arranged for a business purpose.

Subjective organization of business information is according to intrinsic values or characteristics of the data involved. Personnel records, shareholder records, and strategic plans may be organized to establish some desired control or limitation. Personnel records, above all else, must be controlled even though certain elements in them are needed for business processes, such as sending out employee notices and publications. Strategic plans may have great importance to many people, but to protect the business' competitive posture only sections may be released to specified individuals.

Ideally, all the employees should have all the plans, if we expect them to contribute whole-heartedly to accomplishment. But the business environment doesn't allow that, so we use a subjective organization for strategic planning information.

In many instances, information organized objectively is placed in subjective subgroupings for security purposes. Business files on a computer that are protected through the use of passwords are an example. These files may exist on the disk along with "public" files, but their subjective characteristics make it necessary that the information manager deny them to the employees generally.

Information Ownership Concepts

In almost every business of any considerable size there are "resource owners"—not the shareholders or legal owners but conceptual owners, the managers responsible for shepherding a particular resource in the course of operations. The fruit-and-vegetable produce manager at the supermarket is a resource owner. So is the inventory or materials manager in a manufacturing concern, and the buyer in a department store. These are people who have been assigned responsibilities for managing a resource in the best interests of a business. The financial controller is a resource manager of considerable importance.

Data Management

If information is one of the key resources for business in the information age, surely we need information resource managers and, at lower organization levels, "data owners."* The data owner has a number of important responsibilities in the management of the information resource. These include establishing information element definitions, controlling access to and use of information, and authorizing modification and update of information. Usually, these responsibilities are fulfilled through the information management functions, but the primary responsibility remains with the functional manager or data owner. We deal with this in more detail in Chapter 4.

People who say at this point "What a lot of bureaucratic nonsense" should remember that information is not only a critical resource, it is an expensive resource. Major businesses spend hundreds of millions of dollars collecting and processing information, yet the absence of management effort can destroy the efficacy of the information gathered at such cost. A

Information as used here refers to data organized for a purpose; *information elements* or *data* refers to raw items of information stored in a file according to inherent characteristics or relational values.

description of the activities involved in data ownership may clarify the point.

The data owner is usually the manager responsible for the primary purpose of an information file. Or the data owner may be the manager responsible for budgeting for the information system that is the principal user of the particular information file. The data ownership concept is usually limited to a particular well-defined set of data. The data owner of a personnel information file is usually the personnel manager. The data owner for a customer information file is usually the marketing manager or customer administration manager. The exact title is unimportant, but the data owner should be the manager in the best position to make judgments about the organizing, valuation, and use of the information resource, as explained below.

In establishing information element definitions, the data manager

1. Defines clearly the purpose, intent, and meaning of an information element
2. Specifies how the information element is to be developed, and by whom
3. Develops and provides an information storage structure suitable to the perceived uses of the element
4. Authorizes updating, retrievals, and modifications and specifies how and under what conditions these actions may occur
5. Takes all prudent actions to ensure the integrity of the information through security and procedural arrangements.

Figure 3.1 shows how standard data elements provide for more efficient, controlled information use.

A comparison with the processes in a well-managed stockroom will show that these data ownership functions are merely a mirror of those activities which, although mundane, reflect management care for a resource.

Defining Our Terms

Information resource management has a number of aspects, among which are assuring privacy, integrity, and reliability. Some definitions are in order at this point to avoid the confusion all too common in the usual application of the terms.

Integrity refers to the expected qualities of completeness and correctness in business information. Integrity is achieved when good and effective systems and procedure design, employee training, effective supervision, and efficient controls are in place. Information has integrity when it is free from intentional or unintentional errors to the degree expected in normal operations and has not been modified or processed in any unauthorized manner. Security is often a requisite to integrity, but is not a synonym.

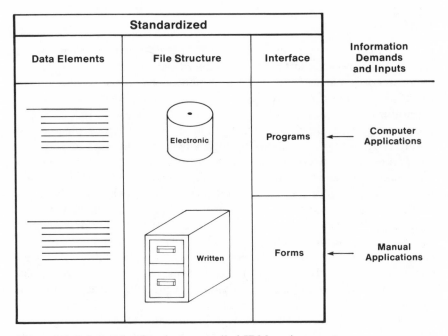

Figure 3.1 Information flow in a controlled IRM environment.

Reliability ensures that the business will always have the information needed to make decisions, when and where required, while integrity relates to data wholeness and freedom from error or improper modification. Reliability refers to the provision of information at the time and place needed. An advantage of electronic information forms is their mobility across time and space. Contingency planning and aspects of security are related to the quest for reliability in business information. In Chapter 10 we address this concern in detail.

Privacy is a condition in which information is protected from observation or uses perceived as inimical to the interests of the subject of that information. Generally, privacy refers to information an individual or business would not wish to have generally exposed. Security is often a necessary contributor to privacy, but is not synonymous with it.

Security is protection from hostile attack, subversion, and espionage and, in the case of information resources, unauthorized modification, destruction, observation, or theft. Reliability and integrity depend on security elements properly applied to meet the vulnerabilities of the business information resource valuation and application situation.

Records Management

Records management is the part of information resource management (IRM) that concerns the formal retention of business documents. An effective records management program minimizes records storage and control costs while meeting all requirements of law and reducing the potential exposures of a business should litigation require a discovery process. Records management should be closely related to contingency planning to ensure continuity of operations through alternative business information generation and recovery practices in event of a serious failure of normal information-processing activities. Records management activities implement the decisions of the data owner in determining who may retain information. And records management functions implement company policies concerning destruction of routine documents; periodic clearing of files; standard organization for paper files and long-term electronic storage files; clearing or sanitizing of electronic files; and retention under controlled conditions for records required by law. In some states and countries, records management also has responsibilities for meeting privacy legislation requirements.

Records management activities deal mostly with subjectively organized information distant from ongoing information processing activities. Generally but not exclusively, the function deals with historical records. With the advent of the information age and the movement of all time-sensitive business data to electronic form, the records management responsibility should be integrated with an overall IRM activity. Security is essential to effective records management.

The data owner responsible for information resource management within the scope of his or her defined task has a complex function. Like the manager of other business resources, he or she tries to provide effective information resources to meet a business function's needs at reasonable cost. The computer is the logical tool to accomplish such a task. Economics thus drives business information resources into electronic forms. In the process the data owner must also ensure that legal, privacy, and integrity requirements are met, so a close working relationship with the security function is necessary.

Most progressive businesses, especially the larger ones, have recognized the importance of information management by appointing a senior executive with overall staff responsibility for the IRM function. The title of such a position may be Vice President/Information Resources or Director/ Information Management. In any case, this executive is responsible for seeing that appropriate data owners are identified in the various organizations and functions and that suitable resources and efforts are directed toward the information management goals outlined above.

Business Information and the Computer

We have seen that information constitutes the critical business resource for the 1980s and beyond. We have also discussed technology's contribution to business competence and seen how technological research and development generates much of the high-value information we are concerned about. There is a reverse twist to this story, however, because one of the products of twentieth-century technology, the ubiquitous computer, is the primary reason for the importance of information. A number of points illustrate the chicken-and-egg relationship between technology and information.

Technology spawned the computer; most technology development today uses the computer as its basic research and development tool.

Information generation mostly concerns technology; the technical information can be published and distributed because of technological developments applying the computer to these tasks.

Information gains in value as its utility increases; information's utility value depends on our ability to develop, collect, organize, store, retrieve, structure, and deliver it. Before the computer, managers were able to handle only very limited, locally stored information sets. Computing technology both generates vast amounts of information and enables us to prepare and deliver it for management purposes. Computers thus contribute to information values if we use them properly; otherwise we may suffer from too much information.

Technology is necessary to develop and deliver more technology. Manufacturing lines for the production of microcircuits are possible only because we have adapted computers to control this process: humans simply could not maintain the tolerances needed. Computers give birth to more sophisticated computers, which in turn—and so on endlessly.

Innovative entrepreneurs in large and small businesses are producing an amazing array of products and services. Most of these are delivered only because of technological innovation that is possible only because of the computer. The innovative knowledge or competence that is the basis for these businesses could not be handled effectively without computer-based information processing and communications.

From these examples we can draw a general rule about the business information resource and the computer; as follows:

The quality and consequently the value of business information increases exponentially with the use of properly designed computing; the demand for computer information services increases exponentially as information quality increases.

Even if our rule is only partly true, the business information resource will become increasingly critical and valuable as a competitive edge. As its value increases, it will become a more attractive target for industrial espionage and malicious attacks. Business managers must have a practical view of our vulnerabilities and our responsibilities for safeguarding information.

Developing technology will affect our business information resource. With technology development proceeding at startling speed, tomorrow is here today.

Changes in technology are driven by economics: microelectronic circuitry and condensation of information storage will provide ever more attractive adaptation of the computer to complement or replace human efforts. During the next decade, computing functions will be determined more by microcode (instructions engineered into the circuitry) than by the traditional programming. Large central computers will represent collections of processors executing specialized functions. Local information resource users will be connected with the central computer and will have convenient, high-level languages and powerful software packages to use to retrieve data for information or for further local processing. Personal computing and communicating workstations will become part of the kit of all professionals, executives, and other knowledge workers. And, artificial intelligence (AI) systems promise to deliver spectacular "assistance" in many decision-making tasks. Networks of intelligent workstations will develop and will spread throughout the business world except to perhaps the very smallest companies.

Computing will be delivered into homes as part of the teletext/television home service package. As various networks develop, integration will become desirable and technically feasible. Just as the telephone network today provides interfaces to allow direct dialing across the world, so information networks will develop. These networks will carry voice and data traffic and will provide services for digitized images as well as television signals. For businesses, these services will tie into automated local exchanges built around the digital PBX (telephone private branch exchange). Increased information storage and retrieval capabilities will result from greatly improved magnetic storage systems and from innovative methods like optical storage.

EDP Analyzer projects that six general levels of information processing will result from applications of this new technology:

1. Corporate headquarters
2. Regional processing centers
3. Site processing centers (plants, warehouses, and the like)
4. Departmental processors
5. Work-group processors
6. Personal workstations. (June 1983, p. 6)

According to *Analyzer*, the top three levels are those that have traditionally had information-processing power. The bottom three are new locations for information resource handling—and are the places where the vast majority of employees work and live.

If we consider the technology developments described and our general rule on technology/information relationships, we can begin to appreciate the implications of

The delivery of information resources and the concurrent transfer of responsibility to individuals (the lower three levels)

The impact of increasing information resource availability and dispersion on control of this resource

The need *now* for management to consider an information resource management commitment.

John Diebold sums it up: "The direction of technology today is such that if you don't focus on information, the technology is irrelevant" (Diebold, 1982). General management or control of the information resource is the essential to establishing information protection.

Managed Information and Business Advantages

Managing the information resource is simply good business; we must manage and control any resource of value to ensure that we obtain maximum benefits from that resource investment. Information resources have unique capabilities, however. Astute information resource management may have important secondary effects on our business. These benefits may include enhancement of our primary business opportunities, diversification into allied lines of business, and the application of specialized information management capabilities to new business activity. Consider these examples, based on actual observations:

● A publishing company developed a highly efficient order-processing and delivery system that used computer terminals at customer procurement offices. This publisher found a new and profitable business venture when the company offered to act as an agent for customers in ordering and delivering bookstore notions and supplies. The information bases already established, along with the systems infrastructure set up for the primary publishing business, provided a ready-made system base for the service.

● A hospital-supply business placed microcomputers in its hospital customers' offices. The information management structure established by the supplier allowed the hospitals suddenly to become much more effective in their own information handling. As a result the supplier's business with the hospitals increased spectacularly.

● An airline developed a passenger information and reservations system; this information was critical to the success of the airline's basic business. In addition, the effectiveness with which the airline managed a vast information resource opened opportunities to sell services to other airlines.

The message in these stories is that business managers should see information resource management not as a necessary reaction to changing times but as an opportunity for real business advantage. In the process of managing an important resource to ensure control of information costs and quality the information manager may also generate new business.

The subsets of IRM—security, records management, and data administration—all have important potentials for increasing business efficiencies and hence profits.

Legal Protection for Business Information

This book deals with managing and safeguarding valuable business information through the identification, marking, and control of information. However, certain types of information may be provided further protection through the application of commonly available legal protections. A brief description of these protections follows. The reader having need to use these methods should consult a qualified lawyer before taking action.

Trade Secrets

Trade secrets are a concept, not a creature of law. But the protection offered to established trade secrets is defined by various laws in most jurisdictions. The courts have created the idea of trade secrets as they ruled in cases that dealt with the concept of fair competition. A trade secret is any piece of information, unknown to others or at least not used by them, that would give a business an advantage over competitors.

A trade secret can usually be defended in court if the matter has not been disclosed otherwise (as in a patent filing), is not widely known or used, is effectively controlled as to release to people inside and outside the business, and has been treated by its owners as a valuable. This last requirement goes directly to the heart of the subject matter of this book: unless business managers handle and protect information as a valuable asset, which implies identification and control, the business may find that it has no legal standing when it tries to recover in court.

Patents

Patents are appropriate only for those processes or formulas that involve an invention; they are not suitable for all kinds of information. Patents require the publication of the information involved, so as to allow the issuance of the patent rights. Patents are good for only seven years and can be invalidated for various reasons, including discovery that a prior patent contains the same ideas. In many cases, the trade secret may be preferable to the patent as a means for protection of information.

Copyright

Copyright is a legal protection for intellectual information that occurs in a particular format or style. For example, there is a valid copyright on this book, even though all the ideas in it can be found elsewhere, although not in the same arrangement. Copyrights are ideal protection for things like books, musical arrangements, and computer software where licensing of hundreds of thousands of users is impractical but where the author wishes to maintain rights.

An excellent reference on the legal aspects of these matters is James Pooley's *Trade Secrets—How to Protect Your Ideas and Assets*, published by Osborne/McGraw-Hill in 1982.

In the next chapter we will look at the concepts of information resource management in detail. We will see what the information resource manager must do to achieve control. We shall consider the business organization and functions related to information management responsibilities.

II | A Management Approach

4 Concepts of Information Resource Management

This information [Resource Management] function must be based on four guiding principles:

- *The integration of content—so that elements from any one data base are available for appropriate combination and manipulation with data elements from other data bases.*
- *The integration of technology so that the machines and systems can talk to one another.*
- *The segmentation of information so that it is unnecessary to pick one's way through the universe of data.*
- *The filtering of information so that the user can selectively access specific, relevant information.*

—Herbert R. Brinberg (1984, p. 8)

In the preceding chapter we discussed the management of the information resource as an important business task. In this chapter we will look in some detail at the concepts of information resource management (IRM).

As a key business resource, the business information "bank" or "pool" deserves recognition and care. Business management must provide the same direction, structure, and control for information it provides for resources like personnel and materials.

The Society for Information Management, in a special 1982 issue of *MIS Quarterly*, discussed the "Future Role of the Information Systems Executive." The authors say that the corporate information officer "will have the responsibility of assuring that new opportunities presented by the technology are seized and that capital expenditures for information resources are ranked according to business needs." Further, the information officer must be a member of top management, not merely an information custodian, but one who "understands the interconnection between the information flow and the business." Responsibilities of the information executive will include corporate data management, networks, data centers, and software development. The conceptual role of the information manager is that of organizer, classifier, maintainer, controller, and deliverer of business information.

Component Activities in Information Resource Management

Information resource management involves these seven principal activities:

1. Defining the business information resource dimensions. What are the information elements that make up the information resource necessary to operate profitably?

2. Valuing the information elements defined as being in the information resource pool. The assigned value determines management's efforts in information control and protection, the same as for other business resources.
3. Establishing information element definitions, to set a clear and consistent meaning across all information systems applications and information uses. Especially where computers are widely used, a lack of definition can result in compromising the integrity and usefulness of management reports.
4. Fix responsibility for control of the various information elements. This responsibility, usually called data administration, includes issuing and canceling authority to establish, change, and use information elements; approving new data elements or revisions to definitions; controlling authority to make updates or changes to the official data element files. Controls as described become more rigorous as information element value increases—again, the same as for other business resources.
5. Determine and set records retention policies and schedules. Usually, these requirements are based on legal obligations. In today's litigious business environment, proper control and timely elimination of records can be critical. Continued management attention is necessary in larger businesses and in those with competitive technology bases.
6. Establish information security policies consistent with information element values and management's risk-taking posture. Develop practical application procedures and publish as standards and, when appropriate, as local procedure. Monitor the efficacy of the information security system through a network of security coordinators or the equivalent. Use risk-analysis methods to evaluate management decisions to accept unusual risks.
7. Plan for contingencies that may threaten continued operability by denying the business its critical information needs. Arrange for alternative resources, back-up information stores, alternative actions, and the like to ensure continuing business viability in the event of a serious information capability loss.

The appendixes offer examples of policy and procedure underlying information resource management.

Defining Information Resource Dimensions

Every business manager uses information. Management may be done through people but decisions should be based on information. Managers are usually very much interested in the timeliness and quality of the information available as a base for decision-making. This concern is a reflection of the information qualities called integrity and reliability and defined in Chapter 3.

Business managers seldom think about the total information resource: What is the minimum essential pool of information necessary to run the business? From a rational conceptual viewpoint, any resource of value should be managed. And to manage something, we must know what it is, its characteristics and boundaries. Yet most business managers (even senior executives in many large companies) have never considered information a resource and have taken no steps to get the information resource under control. They may think of information as some vague, insubstantial, metaphysical good that occurs anywhere and everywhere and will, they hope, be available when needed. These same managers spend vast sums of money in obtaining computer and telecommucations resources to handle this information. Yet, as we saw in Chapter 2, information itself is indeed a most expensive resource.

Most often we find that executives with titles like Director of Information Systems are really managers of vast collections of hardware and millions of lines of software code. That's rather like the diamond manager in a jewelry store being called the Vaults Manager and spending all his or her time worrying about the technology of time locks, tumblers, keys, and alarm systems. The value, of course, is the jewels, not the containers. In business, information is the valuable asset, not the technologies surrounding its use. Most information losses in business, in fact, result from preoccupation with the glamours of technology and the resulting ignorance about and carelessness with the real valuable, the information itself.

To manage a resource, we have to know what that resource consists of. In other words, what are the information elements in our business? Although one seldom finds a business that does not know, within some reasonable margin of error, its levels of raw materials or personnel rosters, most businesses have never even attempted an inventory of their information items. To do so means going through the business and identifying each unique data element; if similar (not necessarily identical) information elements occur more than once, that element should be counted as only one. As an example, consider EMPLOYEE NAME. This is a universal information element, although it may occur in many forms (with full first name, one initial only, perhaps as last name only with employee number, for example), but EMPLOYEE NAME is only one basic element. We need to know all the basic information elements in our particular business. Some of these may be as shown in Table 4.1:

The numbers of unique information elements can be quite large. But unless we know what they are, we cannot begin to put in place controls that will allow us to manage this important resource.

Table 4.1 Typical Unique Information Elements

Employee name and address	Customer accounts
Customer name and address	Sales histories
Shareholder name and address	Field services and repairs
Raw materials (may be multiple items)	Accounts payable
Work in process	Business travel
Finished goods	General ledger
Sales prospects	Engineering data
Orders	Research data
Accounts receivable	

Valuing Information Elements

Knowing the boundaries and contents of the business information resource is a necessary first step but not enough to allow wise management. We must also know the values of the various information elements making up the business information pool or resource. In the management of raw materials, personnel, and engineering the degree of concern and the amount of discretionary spending involved in each relates to the value of the resource item. A high-value resource such as a key executive or a milling machine justifies more management effort (which means larger investment) than that expended for a lower-level employee or a lawnmower.

The same rationale holds for information. Certain types or elements are of very high value, whether defined objectively or subjectively. Others may be of middle-range value, still others of insignificant value. Decisions on management effort should be predicated on the information values assigned as part of the information resource management process. Put another way, we will wish to take much greater pains to protect high-value information than to protect lower-value information. Figure 4.1 illustrates this approach, which is developed more fully in subsequent chapters. Reports on new product developments would be carefully secreted; lists of facility addresses, which may be public knowledge, may require little or no security. Similarly, management of highly valued information elements, perhaps stored in computer data banks, may require intensive care. This care includes decisions about functions, accesses, replication, definition, and the like. The established value of the information alerts information managers to take extra care.

Defining Information Elements

A most important action immediately following the identification of any business' total information resource is the fixing of information element definitions. The computer age has made data definition an important man-

INFORMATION SECURITY PROTECTIVE ELEMENTS

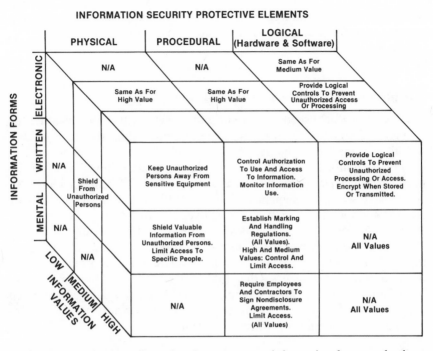

Figure 4.1 Application of security elements across information forms and values.

agement responsibility. As use of computers and networks expands, data may be replicated at various operating sites. New data elements may be generated, with subtle differences resulting from variations in local software programs. The central, or "official," data bases must therefore contain data elements that are clearly defined. The agreed meaning of such basic data elements becomes essential to management control and use of information.

Definition should also establish unique names for the data elements. The element EMPLOYEE PROFILE may be established to mean the employee records in the company standard format, including education and performance appraisals. The term *employee profile* then does *not* mean physical characteristics, although at some unseen future time and place someone may try to make it mean that, with possible confusing results. If local computers should be used to process employee data, reports derived from unchanged data extracted from the data base could be labeled "From Employee Profile data." However, if the data are changed in any way through processing against local programs, that claim could not be used.

Information-element definitions are like the labels required on food products; they tell users what they are getting and avoid confusion resulting from replicated information elements that may incur different shades of meaning because of different handling of processing. This aspect becomes critical when local or personal computing may result in unplanned, uncontrolled processing.

Establishing Information Control Responsibility

We have now established a set of information elements that constitute the business information resource; we have assigned values (in terms of classifications rather than dollars, pounds, or the like) to these elements and provided definitions so that each unique information item has a precise meaning (which also limits the characteristics of that information element). As we have seen, the element EMPLOYEE PROFILE must contain *only* the items in the official company employee record.

With that done, we can now describe the control responsibility or management process involved. The first steps (organizing and valuing) were necessary to supply the responsible managers enough information about the information resource so that they can manage it. Managing means controlling and protecting and applies to information management much as to management of other resources essential to business operations. Information resource management controls include:

1. Establishing controls over access to high-value information in all forms. This may include information in mental form, in documents, and in computer data bases.
2. Setting and enforcing requirements for authorization to access information. Subauthorities include rights to read only, modify, operate a program, transfer, extract, and so on. These are the privileges described under Access Management in Chapter 6.
3. Issuing, canceling, and monitoring authorizations to access or use information. These authorizations may be personal, departmental, or for other business entities that have a need for information. For high-value data, the default option (action taken automatically if no direction has been provided) must always be to deny access. We should note here that this function of controlling access to information has a great potential for management cost control. Years ago, while in the military, I asked a manager for his copy of a huge report I had seen being distributed only the day before. To his chagrin, the report was fished from the trash. Although he had no need for it, he feared that a cancellation would indicate a loss of status. An effective control over rights to information can cut administrative and data-processing costs.

Such management of the information resource is a recognition that information use entails enormous expenditures. The key to control is not through management of hardware and software (although that effort is laudable) but through definition and authorization of business use of information itself.

The establishment of effective management control over the use of information can provide important business advantages, among them:

1. Improved control over the costs of information systems development and operation. In the early years of commercial data processing user departments developed requirements without regard for existing data-file structures or data pools. As a result, new systems often replicated data elements already found in other systems, and software was developed which duplicated other general-purpose software for which the business was already paying depreciation charges. Information resource management offers the chance to gain control of the information resource and thus stop duplication and redundancy in the myriad applications and information-generation activity that goes on in most modern businesses. Even in smaller companies, the use of a master information plan can reduce data-systems development costs and maintain an overall information structure that will be both easier to use and more cost effective.

2. By ensuring consistency of meaning and use, and avoiding controllable redundancies in information uses, information resource management can encourage optimal use of distributed processing and personal workstation automation. As information spreads through the organization, some overall control is essential if the results are to be directed to business goals. An excess of information elements and definitions can be costly and confusing; the current rapid increase in the use of personal computing, networks, and the resulting replication of information items threatens a tide of information outputs. Management needs to establish some controls now; these controls must be reasonable in light of the business' operating mode and goals and should recognize that an effort at microcontrol is neither desirable nor practical. But at the macro level, control of the basic information resource is essential.

Proper Records Retention

Every business has certain records that must be retained for fixed periods of time: fiscal documents, records of ownership, certain classes of financial transactions, and tax records all have various proprietorship and/or legal requirements for retention. In addition, business managers should wish to retain sufficient records in a secure place to allow reconstitution of the business operation in the event of a disaster.

The information resource manager should be in control of the records retention program. This ties in closely with the responsibility for providing contingency planning described in Chapter 10. A careful analysis of the company's legal, fiscal, and ownership obligations is the preliminary step in developing a records retention scheme. Since records of past decisions may be found and used, perhaps to the company's detriment in legal proceedings (the discovery process), an important part of a records management program is the *destruction* of records as soon as practical business needs and legal requirements allow. Employees, especially company officers and legal counsel, should be discouraged from packing away notes and memoranda in personal files for long periods of time.

An effective records system means that

1. Only required records are maintained after the minimum business requirement period expires (typically, one year).
2. Records retention arrangements provide for orderly, clean, safe storage, permitting efficient retrieval when needed.
3. Records retained are identified to the proprietorship, legal, fiscal, or other authoritative requirement being satisfied.
4. Expired records are promptly removed from retention storage and destroyed.
5. Working records storage (such as filing cabinets in offices, tape libraries in data centers) is purged periodically and records destroyed or sent to permanent storage. Usually such action is on an annual cycle.

Records management should not be a casual and desultory effort; these records can be critical should a lawsuit or disaster occur.

Proper Information Security

A significant portion of this book deals with securing information. As we already know, security is an important part of the information management responsibility. Security is essential to information integrity and reliability, important qualities if the business is to rely on its information for decision-making. Security interfaces closely with such other information management responsibilities as records management and contingency planning. Security therefore cannot be delegated away; it must be closely integrated with the overall information resource management planning and control. The information access decisions described rely in large part on security measures for control; since almost all time-sensitive business information is in electronic form today, effective logical (nonphysical) access security controls are essential for information management. Figure 4.2 shows how IRM ensures information quality.

Contingency Planning

Any well-managed business has contingency plans for various situations that might affect the availability of labor, capital, raw materials, parts, transportation, and so on. Certainly the information resource deserves

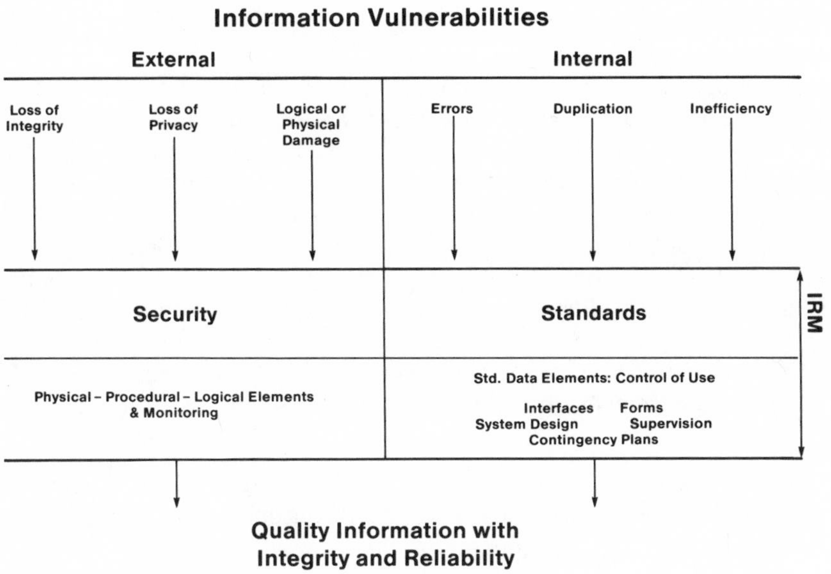

Information Vulnerabilities

External			Internal		
Loss of Integrity	Loss of Privacy	Logical or Physical Damage	Errors	Duplication	Inefficiency

Security	Standards
Physical – Procedural – Logical Elements & Monitoring	Std. Data Elements: Control of Use Interfaces Forms System Design Supervision Contingency Plans

IRM

Quality Information with Integrity and Reliability

Figure 4.2 IRM controls ensure information quality.

equal management attention. Unfortunately, managers often think of information as an intangible and therefore unmanageable. (In Chapter 10 we discuss reliability planning, which involves other information management activities such as security and records retention.) Careful planning can provide for information emergencies, and management should make sure that such planning is done. The best way is through the information resource manager, who has the best overview of the business information needs and circumstances.

Information Resource Management (IRM) is a *major management responsibility* in the information age. IRM has significant tasks that are essential for all businesses, but especially for those in high-technology industries. Top management must take actions *now* to begin the process of managing information. Brian Hollstein, Chairman of the Committee for Safeguarding Proprietary Information of the American Society for Industrial Security, suggests that top management form an "Intellectual Assets Management Council" with high-level representation from research, engineering, marketing, and the like. This idea is exemplary of the kind of management thinking sorely needed in the information age. (Immediate information management actions are discussed in Chapter 11; it will be useful to look ahead at Figure 11.1, which shows IRM organization and functions.) In Chapter 5 we will look at the ways in which technology makes the tasks easier; technology not only drives us to install information resource management, it also makes the job possible.

Personnel Requirements

In most businesses the concepts of information management will be new. If a good job is to be done, some significant training and possibly hiring are needed. We noted in Chapter 1 that most business managers act as though information were free. We have seen that it is not; indeed, it is a very expensive and critical resource. The managers assigned to control this resource must have the background and understanding to prepare them to cope with information in all its forms. Here is a basic set of information skills necessary for those who will manage the information resource:

Information science, the body of knowledge that deals with the ordering and management of information. Library science is a subset of this field.

Systems methodology (not the same as computing science), which deals with the practical application of systems concepts to business problems. Computer-science majors seldom have these skills.

Computing and telecommunications technologies, which include the various technical components and processes involved in computers and communications systems.

Using some of the job titles suggested in this book, we can apply appropriate skills and build a knowledge requirement.

The senior information resource executive should have a broad knowledge of the business and an understanding of macrosystems concepts. This executive should understand that various systems may be appropriate for information handling requirements and that in many cases these systems may involve microforms or manual processes rather than computers. This executive should also have competence in the general application of computers. A manager whose entire background is in data processing may not be best for this position because such people tend to think only in terms of technology application rather than in the broad efficiency-based concepts needed.

Data administration requires a detailed knowledge of the construction and use of data bases. A working familiarity with the data-processing practice and organization in the business is essential. Broad systems analysis competence would be a plus.

Information security should include experience in data processing as an essential prerequisite. An understanding of information science and the operations of the business are helpful.

Systems analysts in the business concerned with information costs should have a broad background, including the application of noncomputing solutions to information-handling problems.

Based on observation of many current companies, here are three minimum requirements for starting up an effective information resource management program:

1. Train the systems analysis staff to consider applications demands against manual processing capabilities as well as against computing methodologies. Many times microforms or various "old-fashioned" methods will provide results superior to those obtained using computers.
2. Train physical security managers and computer security managers to recognize information itself as a critical and valued asset.
3. Train auditors to view information as a controllable resource and to review information management practices in the course of routine audits.

Other employees or new hires who may require information management training are records managers, office managers, and functional managers assigned responsibilities as data owners in terms of our suggested structure for information valuation and control.

5 | Computer Technology and Information Resource Management

Computing has revolutionized business operations and almost all time-sensitive business information is now in electronic form. But this *automation* of business information has not only made information resource management important, it has literally made IRM possible and convenient.

The convenience results from the homogeneity of information in electronic forms. Homogeneity or uniformity of structure means that business managers can make decisions about rules of structure and use of information that can be reasonably applied. In simpler times, business information was gathered in written forms. These forms were so diverse and so difficult to communicate and replicate that any management effort was necessarily local. In a sizable business with all information written on papers, any effort to manage information was a Sisyphean task. There was simply no way to effect control; a limited amount of standardization was achieved through the use of forms. But it remained for the electronic age to deliver the tools for real control.

In a famous 1979 article called "Managing the Crisis in Data Processing" in the *Harvard Business Review* Richard L. Nolan described the stages of development for business information processing. (Figure 5.1 is based on Nolan's projections.) It is generally believed that for most businesses the early 1980s represent the integration stage, in which interfaces between business planning and information technology will be formalized. The next stage includes use of information structures such as data bases and the recognition of information as a critical resource by management. The growing use of personal computing facilities makes the need for such structure critical for today's businesses.

Information Processing Development Stages

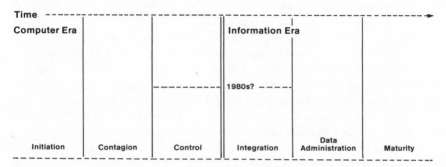

Figure 5.1 Stages of information systems development. (Adapted from Richard L. Nolan, *Harvard Business Review*, March–April 1979.)

Design of Information Systems

Because the computer is essential for information resource management, we must look at the design of computer business systems to appreciate how information management can affect our control over business information resources. From the beginning of commercial application of computing in the 1950s and 1960s until 1970, systems designers provided separate sets of information elements (or files) for each application. A payroll system required that the user set up a file for employee name and number, one for hours worked, one for check addresses, and so forth—and these files were used only in the payroll system. Another system, perhaps involving medical records, used a separate file containing employee name, another containing medical history, and so on. If we consider the information resource important enough to attempt managing it, we quickly conclude that this duplication of information elements (such as employee name) in various files is inherently wasteful, susceptible to errors, and basically uncontrollable. We can refer to these types of information structures as nonintegrated. Another way to describe them would be to use the terms *unmanaged* or *unmanageable*. To manage our information resource, we must use technology to design information systems properly for user control and efficiency.

Steps in designing effective information resource management systems are:

1. Define the basic information types in the business. Usually these will relate directly to the various functions: billing information, payables information, employee information, manufacturing-in-process information, raw materials information.

2. Segregate the information types into unique information elements; only one of each element will be allowed. New elements must be approved by the company's information manager to avoid redundant costs for storage and the errors inherent in unnecessary data replication. The business information manager would set up one master file for each unique information element and by the design of that file establish a method for all the functional systems to extract the information as needed. One extremely important benefit is obvious immediately: a unique information element will always be the same no matter where it appears. A valuation decision about this file means that the particular information will be protected appropriately. Subsequent information valuation decisions may result in assigning different values to functional information sets that contain unique elements such as customer name and address. As an example:

   Customer name and address master file: Mid value

   Customer name/products sold file: High value

   Customer name/ship-to-address for one region: Low value

3. Design a data-systems architecture to make optimum use of the business information resources and to serve business needs best. This activity includes logical (software) design, physical systems design (procedures), and the use of systems design tools such as specialized software for creating computer programs and for managing data structures (file organizations).
4. The general structure for information developed by the information manager becomes the "data dictionary," a formal outline of the data elements authorized for use in the business.

Benefits From Information Structure and Technology

Business managers want useful and timely information upon which to base decisions. Traditional data-processing approaches have failed because the business environment is too dynamic to allow for the long-lead-time system-development processes typical of the past twenty years. Now managers are asking for fast, do-it-yourself capabilities using the so-called fourth-generation languages. (These languages are Englishlike structures that can be used with very little training and that have powerful capabilities for retrieving and structuring data.) Of course the capability to use such retrieval languages assumes that the business has done some planning and has control of the information resource base used in the business.

We are seeing an explosion of software development, especially in programs for the personal computer. This has resulted, in most part, from hardware manufacturers' willing reception of outside-developed software for their computers. The new software is innovative, powerful, and convenient to use. Proper structure in the business' data bases is vital to our being able to make effective use of the new software packages and to allow us to maintain control of our information base during multiple-user accesses and processes.

Database management systems (DBMSs) represent the application of computing technology to the problem of information resource management. Computers with large file-storage subsystems, usually disks, allow management to store information in organized fashion to make updating, access, and delivery efficient and economic. The technologies of file storage are rapidly delivering high-density fast-retrieval capabilities providing for billions of bits of storage in relatively little space. The laser disk is an example of such new developments. Organizational theories such as tree structure and relational structure provide tools for information organization and retrieval vastly superior to anything used twenty years ago.

Building the Data Base

An efficiently designed structure is vital to successful application of computing to the problem; one giant, monolithic data base is hardly ever desirable. A great deal of design work is needed to structure a DBMS suitable to the business. Design work logically follows definition of the basic information element set.

Difficulties in implementing a DBMS are often chiefly political and organizational. Taking advantage of a DBMS usually requires that management reorganize and in the process create some new information resource jobs. Top management must realize that (1) information is a resource, clearly distinguishable from its users and processors; (2) information needs managing; and (3) proper planning and design can provide computer systems for effective management utilization of and control over the information resource.

The information management structure is always more important than the technical structure of the data management program. While the DBMS allows the data to be considered separately from uses and applications programs, the dynamics of modern business assure that the information manager cannot reasonably expect to achieve total standardization. The years required to build a system that fully integrates all business functions are just too costly in terms of lost opportunity and resistance to change. By the time such a system is built, the business environment has developed into a different model, and the DBMS will no longer fit.

The business information manager must therefore bite off the information apple one piece at a time. While the goal remains standardization and efficiency of information use, various requirements may indicate that, for practical purposes, several distinct database systems are appropriate.

These database systems may be homogeneous groupings of information elements. For example, the database systems in a large manufacturing business might include

Engineering data base—product concept, design, and documentation.

Manufacturing data base—production, cost, planning, and build control information.

Personnel data base—employee records, medical records, and payroll information.

Customer administration data base—orders, deliveries, installs, recoveries, service information, accounts receivable, and customer account status information.

The business information manager can begin to obtain control of the information resource by identifying and authorizing appropriate, unique data elements for the various DBMSs. Some redundancy may occur initially; over the longer run the target should be to establish one authorized data element set.

Each data base may have a separate staff for control. This staff, usually called data administration, should be systems-competent but is more closely allied with functional managers than with the information systems staff. The data administration function is replicated for each major business functional DBMS. The business information resource manager may have direct-line control over these groups but usually has staff cognizance (a dotted line).

Usually, such a group will include a data administrator, the chief of the activity (see Figure 5.2); several data analysts for development of suitable information architectures and organizational schemas; data management system coordinators, who implement the plan and keep the data base "tuned" to business needs; and miscellaneous clerical help to record new data elements and keep the data dictionary current. (The data dictionary is the official listing of information elements and their characteristics.)

The data administrator can call upon a wide range of computer software functions to assist in the process of controlling information. A proper use of these software tools can provide an environment with a synergism, so that processing will generate information packaged, presented, and delivered in optimal fashion. These software tools include

Business modeling systems that help the data administrator in designing information-file structures congruent to the business itself.

Packaged software to provide immediate, tested answers to identified business information problems by retrieving and processing data elements and delivering answers to management.

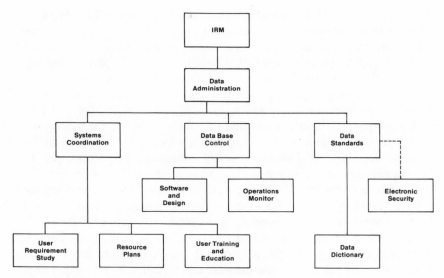

Figure 5.2 Data administration organization.

So-called fourth-generation languages that allow the personal computer-using executive to call out information from the data base system directly or to create minisystems for local purposes.

Modeling tools for development of logical data structures.

Data-dictionary software to support the data element identification, authorization, organization, structure, and access-control activity performed by the DBMS coordinators.

Database Software

A major element in the information management process is of course the database management software itself. Several new applications flow from information resource management; these use the powerful software built to implement IRM. When business information is properly managed and structured (through use of the data dictionary and database technology), the fourth-generation languages bring information tools to the business end-user managers. The tools guide these information users in directly accessing, retrieving, manipulating, and producing usable management information. IBM calls this concept the information center.

The information center constitutes the information user's side of the IRM activity. IRM produces an organized, nonredundant, reliable, secure information store. The business information manager provides systems technology support for both formal and informal retrieval and use of the information resource. The formal information retrieval activity is through the traditional applications systems design functions. The informal or direct accesses to the information resource are through the information center. The information manager provides technical advice and assistance to end-users (frequently those with personal computers; see Chapter 2) who wish to access the data base directly.

Potentially, users may be provided a distributed system—one that connects various user terminals with various information storage and processing computers—in such a way that they do not concern themselves with the location of the data. In providing such services technology is an enabler to better decisions based on more current, more available information, but the requirement for information management becomes ever more acute.

One subject of much current software discussion is the Decision Support System (DSS). Usually, DSS involves the "information center" concept and encompasses a set of powerful, user-friendly software that allows end-users to select services or design and operate minisystems, using personal computers or terminals. DSSs may provide single-key functions for executives; in such a case, prepared software can be called by pressing a single identified-function key on a device, thereby generating a report.

In addition to supporting general classes of end-users, the information center may also be organizationally and/or technically aligned with operations research, office systems design and services, financial modeling and analysis, and shared personal computing resource centers.

Information management (and information security measures) are preconditions to the use of all the innovative, attractive applications. The business that rushes into the use of information centers and other personal information services without first conceptualizing the information resource is headed for disaster.

Some problems the use of such systems is already making evident are the weakening of internal control systems (since data may be replicated); erroneous conclusions on the part of end-users because they assume a quality of information integrity locally processed information may not have; and a risk to basic information-element integrity if users accidentally or purposefully change central master files.

Consider the information-center concept in the light of the proliferation on personal computers, workstations, LANs, and so forth. It is already evident that we will have an increasing vulnerability in these many and informal accesses to our business data base. Here is the chicken-and-egg problem again. Without information resource management, we don't have an information structure for direct user access using the information center concept. Once we do have such access, the information-valuation part of the information-resource-management function becomes critical. It is critical because we must be able to manage the informal accesses to our business data base to maintain security. And security is necessary if we are to ensure data integrity and reliability.

Along with the useful power of the fourth-generation languages, personal computer/workstation users can apply an array of communications features. Most of the new professional workstations and personal computers derive major benefits from communications capabilities. The user can move information from central data bases, send files to other users or to shared files or printers, look at data from one or more distant files concurrently with other users, and so on. In large businesses, these capabilities greatly improve the process of concurrence; in engineering activities, for example, communications power in the new systems allows several engineers to "sign off" on versions of engineering documents at the same time, and if changes are required, electronic distribution reduces the review time significantly. An information management problem is evident here. Information can be replicated in many places by various users; the replications may be processed against individually designed programs, thus resulting in several different versions of the information. Unless the information manager specifies the standard version of the information (recall our earlier discussion of the data dictionary and data definitions) and standard versions of processing software, management may be swamped with conflicting information, each version having its own apostolate with plenty of proofs at hand.

This is not at all to say that users should not retrieve information and process it locally—that is the beauty of the personalization of computing. The information manager must nevertheless make certain that management knows which version of information is sanctioned: that is, which version comes from the data base and software having the imprimatur of the information resource manager. To a large degree, of course, this depends on establishing effective practices for information use. Report titles should be published and the use of those titles restricted to specified circumstances. A periodic summary of operating results should have a unique title to differentiate it from reports that may be produced by local financial analysts. In addition, the use of that title should be reserved to the central data-processing center or headquarters analysts responsible for producting the official version each month. Thus we see that the information resource management activity becomes rather broad, including defined data elements, defined data files, controlled access to and use of these items, and controlled report titles. Whenever we see the word *controlled* we have a potential application for security elements.

Computing and Information Security

Technology feeds the information bank of mankind; this information bank results in ever more technology. Technology fuels the competitive business race for innovation and product value. This same technology offers the chance for a marked improvement in the effectiveness of efforts to protect information and to guarantee privacy and secrecy.

Properly designed computer information systems, as already noted, can provide information with security superior to that which paper-based systems can offer. Well-designed computer systems can establish security measures that

Automatically keep detailed records of all accesses to information (name, authentication, date, time, information items seen or processed, and so on).

Store all information in encrypted form, thus denying the information to unauthorized parties who may obtain the encrypted files but cannot read without the key. The information can be automatically converted to intelligible form when an accessor uses the key.

Allow secure transmission over networks by using encryption. The information can be automatically coded as it passes through a "black box" into the network and returned to clear text when it arrives at its destination.

Establish identification and authentication means far superior to those offered by traditional methods. Technology allows positive identification through the use of effective, unforgeable proofs. An example of such a token is the "smart card." These indentification tokens use microprocessor technology to imbed an encrypted password or ID number in a plastic card. The card contains a picture of the user, plus a magnetically encoded identifier. When entered into the access management system, the microprocessor triggers an identification question-and-answer sequence. The user must know a secret identification number that, in conjunction with possession of the card, provides a strong identity claim. The microprocessor on the card can also be used to store data about selective authorities granted to the bearer, such as approvals to enter certain areas, to access certain files, and the like. (Variations on this theme are almost limitless.) Once the identification claim is made, authentication can be done using extremely precise measurements of physical characteristics—fingerprint scanners, hand-geometry measurement devices, and eye-retina scanners. These methods are virtually foolproof and are far more rigorous and effective than, for example, a picture ID card.

Segregate and selectively issue or control information by function. Authorized information accessors can be precisely controlled in terms of what information may be accessed and what may be done once access is achieved. Properly identified and authenticated persons may be restricted to seeing only one information element; or they may be allowed a full range of services, including processing information against programs. Electronic information technology allows much more precise restriction on information use than does a traditional information-control system; once a person has access to files containing printed documents, it is difficult to prevent most actions against that file, including copying, or perusing unrelated items. Electronic information can be selectively protected in very effective ways.

So we must recognize that, although unrestrained use of computer information systems does create vulnerabilities, proper system design can provide excellent controls ensuring security. The problem of course is in the cost of such controls. Business invests in information technology to provide information delivery systems; we want to make information more available to those who need it. Controls seem to run contrary to this purpose.

This is where proper information-resource valuation becomes so important. The business that has valued and assigned classifications to its information resources has established the basis for good information systems design. Figure 4.1 shows the process of selecting various control levels based on information values.

IRM offers many advantages to a business apart from the security benefits. It represents a viewpoint that considers technical implementation tools as essentials. The tools are not necessary for the concept to exist, but putting IRM ideas into practice without technology would be very difficult. A brief look at some cases illustrating the benefits will be helpful in understanding why IRM is a much wider and more important subject than information security.

Cases

The rationale used by business managers in two cases may help to illustrate how information system technology can provide increased control over valuable business information resources.

Case M

M Company maintained shareholder records on ledgers in the company secretary's office. The records were kept locked in a vault when they were not in use. Although the room in which the work of updating and changing shareholder records was done was reasonably secure, the records were spread out at times. The security was typical of that in a big office building. Strangers were not usually seen, but there was a potential that someone could get in. M Company considered the shareholder records extremely sensitive information.

M decided to automate the process of maintaining shareholder records, mostly as an efficiency move but also to improve security for the records and their processing. The records would be concerted to magnetic form, then encrypted for storage on tape. All processing and storage would be done within the M Company data center, which had rigorous security. Changes were to be entered via forms prepared at the secretary's office and sent to the data center by mail. There they would be keyed into the shareholder system. Printing and handling of output reports, dividend statements and checks, and proxy solicitations were to be done in a special area, using the procedures developed for payroll processing. Delivery and mailing of reports and statements was to be handled by special M Company messengers, with receipts. Audit controls built into the system ensured serial-number control of documents and batch control of inputs and outputs.

M Company was able to identify a number of security benefits from the conversion to the automated system, and efficiency was increased markedly. Some of the security benefits were:

1. Shareholder-record files were stored in encrypted form and maintained in a high-security area. They were considered as having very little exposure to physical attack or attempts at physical information theft. There was practically no way for anyone to get at the entire file. The encryption key was maintained by one employee and the job set up to process had to be done by other people.
2. Processing and printing were done under control of job tickets and were supervised in a special high-security environment. Audit and control steps were built in to ensure accuracy. Several different groups of people had to be involved in each step, making collusion unlikely.

The benefits to the shareholders include more accurate and timely accounting.

Case T

T Corporation built a new research center. T management determined at the start that this would be a "paperless" center. All records would be maintained on microforms or on magnetic media. There would be no storage of laboratory notebooks, research reports, or the like. As research papers were generated they were converted to computer information forms if used for current projects. If to be stored for reference, they were converted to microforms. Paper documents were destroyed after the replacements were proofed.

Electronic documents were stored on a closed network within the research center. Microforms were stored and controlled by the research center library. Reports could be issued to approved research staff on a receipt basis; printouts could be made if approved by senior staff members. The primary reason for this approach was to avoid the piles of paper traditional in a research environment and to make information readily available to research staff. But security benefits, important to protect the T company's investment in technology, were evident.

1. Access to information could be restricted to fit circumstances. In cases where discovery information was critical to the business, access control systems for both electronic and microform storage could be used to grant access selectively. Individual access rights could be modified as assignments changed or as people joined or left the research staff.
2. The stored information was more secure; an unauthorized person entering the research center would have to break through the electronic security barriers or the vault and container locks for the microforms. Had the information been in written form, on paper, the bulk of it would have meant that most would be on shelves, available to a miscreant.

These cases show how information security can be improved by using modern information processing technology. Vulnerabilities exist for information in any form. But the use of computers and personal workstations does not necessarily mean increased risk. When properly designed and installed, electronic information systems can improve efficiency *and* security.

We begin once more to see how the issue at hand is not computer-related crime but rather the management of information. And we can envision how managing information will provide our business with security and other benefits which are equally important. Figure 5.3 shows the development of the technology infrastructure over time, supporting information handling. All parts of the structure, including the central processor servicing the data bases, are developing in capability at an astonishing rate.

Continuing Evolution of the Computing Infrastructure

Although some information-processing activities in business are properly performed without using computers (examples include forms applications and the use of microfilm systems), the computer and its ancillary devices make up the primary information-processing infrastructure today. Almost all time-sensitive business information (which includes almost all data used in managing) is now in electronic form, at least in some part of its life cycle. The frequency and pervasiveness of computer use is due in part to its attractiveness as a means for providing efficiency. A far greater impetus comes from the economics of computing, where increasingly more powerful, smaller, and cheaper devices are proving to be indispensable helps to knowledge workers.

Against this bright view we must recognize a set of braking factors, problems that can put a serious hold on attempts to move rapidly into the most advanced information-gathering and delivery processes.

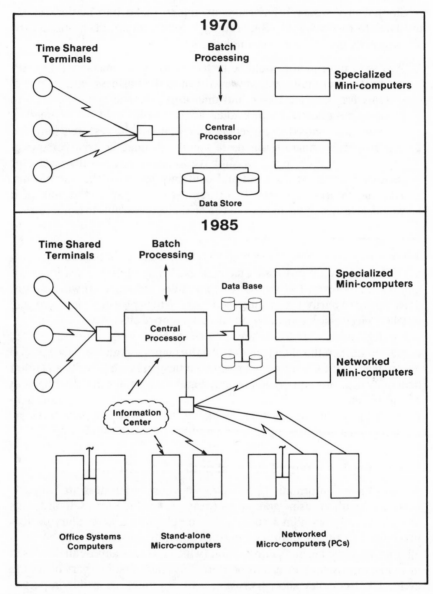

Figure 5.3 Stages of development in information infrastructure.

1. The existing applications code investment (currently used programs) represents billions of lines of program instructions, mostly tuned to old technology. These programs have been written over the past twenty years; although the applications could be done better and the computers

would run more efficiently if the programs were rewritten, the cost of such an effort is clearly unacceptable from a business-cost viewpoint. Clearly, an immediate move into the full panoply of IRM technologies would be inappropriate for most businesses.

2. To compound the problem, many of the data files retrieved by the old programs are not efficiently organized so as to make use of modern database storage and retrieval technology. Many of the file structures are unique to a particular business application. The standard interface demanded for efficient mass storage and retrieval techniques cannot be used.

3. An enormous backlog of unfulfilled systems development and maintenance requests has built up across most businesses. This is a complex problem. Old systems absorb large amounts of programming resources to maintain them in effective operating condition. These resources are not then available to reprogram the systems into more efficient postures that would allow the use of recent database technology. Further, the fast pace of today's highly competitive, technologically oriented business environment means that business managers are insatiably developing new demands for information systems services. Proper implementation of IRM concepts would do much to alleviate the load problem, but most businesses do not have the resources to do so. The popularity of information centers, personal computing, and distributed computing services have as a base this inability to meet management information service needs through traditional data processing structures.

6 | Controlling and Securing Information Through Effective Information Resource Management

The speed of change in the technology of information processing and utilization has made it very difficult for an adequate level of competence to be maintained in the many divisions and functions into which most large companies are subdivided. Thus, the chief information officer has as a primary function the responsibility of providing consulting services to the operating divisions and functions. The corporate accounting/finance function and the corporate certified public accountants audit the accuracy *of financial records. Similarly, the chief information officer should be responsible for audits of the* effectiveness and efficiency *of information processing and utilization.*

—W. R. Synott and W. H. Gruber (1981, p. 12)

Now we can consider how to put together a coherent information resource management program that will reflect our management's risk-taking posture, a fair information valuation, and practical, appropriate, and economic information control and security investment.

The Information Resource Management Framework

The general concept and management structure upon which an information security program must be constructed is that of information resource management (IRM). IRM reflects a management recognition that current, reliable, quality business information is an important resource essential to successful operation. To attempt to develop and implement a business information security program without acceptance of IRM as a valid management concept is foolish if not foolhardy. Effective security depends on correct information value assignments. Information valuation flows from a recognition of information as a critical business asset—or, by another name, IRM. There is no well-defined, always-appropriate procedure for establishing IRM as a business function. However, based on practical insights and experience, we can suggest some natural decision processes and sequential activities that will begin the evolution of such a program for a large business. Smaller businesses will reflect some appropriate subset. Figure 6.1 illustrates an organizational structure and functional placement for IRM. The most effective placement for the information-protection activity is within the business' security department. Consider which other

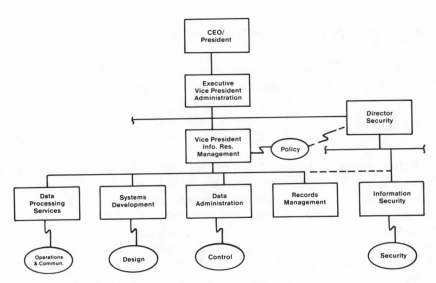

Figure 6.1 IRM organization and assignment of functions.

business resources are managed by functional executives but protected by the security activity.

The traditional information systems and information processing organization has changed little. However, it now reports into a major management function and assumes its rightful role as processor, not keeper, of information. Systems development functions become simplified as standard definitions and interfaces are provided for the key information elements in the business. Information systems take on a strategic role as a high-level management purview allows better planning for the use of information as an important business leverage. Information can be a competitive tool, and imaginative business use of computers and information can increase sales and improve organizational effectiveness. More to the point here, IRM will provide the essentials for a practical approach to providing the security for valuable business information.

The first essential step is *recognition of information resource management as an important business responsibilty*. In a small to medium-size business, this recognition of IRM may be no more than a discussion by management of the valuable information used and which elements require special management effort. In larger businesses, and certainly in any business with a high-technology basis, formal IRM responsibilities should be assigned. It is important to be practical. Consider the management attention given to other important business resources such as personnel and inventories, then organize for IRM in a manner that makes sense for you.

Putting a Value on Business Information

The old adage "knowledge is power" is coming to have its commercial counterpart in the more crass but equally valid aphorism "information is money." In a nation that is entering the so-called postindustrial information society, information has quite literally become capital. (Spanner, 1984)

Before anyone can make decisions about managing a resource, information about the value of the thing or person to be managed must be at hand. An example might be the use of personal safe-deposit boxes. If you do not know the value of your belongings you will have difficulty in determining what to put in the box. You obviously can't put everything you own in a safe-deposit box. So you must decide what is most valuable, either in terms of intrinsic value (such as diamonds) or sentimental value (love letters).

It is surprising that many business managers embark on a program for information management without determining information values. As is the case with a safe-deposit box and personal articles, the business cannot protect all information effectively. The costly and therefore limited management effort must be applied selectively, and to do so intelligently one first needs a valuation of all business information.

In almost all cases, some very small portion of the total information resource will be extremely valuable, worth taking rigorous measures to control and protect. Some larger number of information elements will require an effective but more general management effort. Finally, the major part of the business information resource will be of a value that requires only a rule against publication unless officially announced.

Information valuation is an important part of the information resource management process. Almost all of the data owner's responsibilities require that he or she be aware of the value of the information being managed. How else to make rational decisions about sharing and access rules?

Making Value Decisions

A requirement for making information value decisions is a knowledge of the working of the business, especially the functional, operations-related aspects. How is the information used? The data owner is usually in a functional business activity, typically the one having primary use of the data. We can thus assume some familiarity with functional information applications and a capability to value data in line with its importance to the ongoing business. In Chapter 3 we discussed the forms and types of business information, categories that are helpful in making value decisions.

A second need for information valuation is an understanding of any legal requirements or exposures under law that might result were the information being valued to be compromised or improperly used. The privacy of personnel records is a good example of such concern; other legal requirements exist in such areas as shareholder accounting, development of income data before earnings announcements, and strategic plans. Remember that security is a necessary element to the qualities of integrity and reliability and privacy, these being responsibilities of the data owners.

Information (*data* in its raw forms) may be assigned value based on subjective or objective criteria. In addition, legal requirements may dictate information-valuation decisions. Subjective valuation depends on qualities inherent in the information itself. For example, personal records may be relatively unimportant to the ongoing operation of the business but require a high valuation because of the need for privacy. They may contain information the average person would not wish to have disclosed. Similarly, results of pure research may not have any direct relationship to business operations but may deserve a high valuation because of their cost or because of their potential for future competitive posture.

Financial data also may have significant subjective value. A business transferring large amounts of money by wire or computer network message would wish to be assured that the message will not be tampered with. The information in the message represents value in itself. In this case, the protective measures have as a goal the integrity but not the privacy of the message. Encryption would seem to be an ideal security measure for this purpose.

Information may also be valued on objective criteria: the importance of the particular data to business operations. Receivables, customer information, inventory data, market strategy, pricing strategy, and product formulas are all information items that might merit high valuation. The question here is what would happen to the business were specific information to be exposed, modified, or destroyed in some unauthorized manner.

Finally, the manager valuing information must consider legal requirements for protection and retention. A policy statement may set forth the general ground rules for making this type of information-valuation decision. In some instances policy defines absolutely the value of a particular data element, file, or class. Usually, however, the manager determining the value of an information item must make an intelligent decision based on business judgment, with the policy providing a structure for the decision and following data-ownership actions.

From a practical point of view, information-valuation decisions may be made by a central appointed authority such as the information management executive. Or they may be made by specified data owners—who, as we have seen, are usually functional managers responsible for the activity having primary use for the data. When information elements pass from one system or domain to another, value decisions may have to be reconsidered. Combining information elements may change the value and indicate a need for increased protection. Finally, in some cases in today's environment, personal computer users, network users, and others doing local or personal processing may have to make on-the-spot decisions concerning newly developed information so that protection will occur simultaneously with the generation of the data. This is especially critical where personal computing and use of networks may expose new and sensitive information unless system users take protective actions.

The organizational placement of valuation responsibility depends on the size and scope of the business. However, it is essential that it be done at the earliest possible stages of information management—usually at the data-definition phase of systems project development, at the generation step where distributed computing is allowing personal access and processing, or where an employee creates a new document.

Valuing Business Information

Information valuation is not a trivial task. The most important thing is to establish a firm base, which means an authoritative decision setting general categories of valuation and their definitions. This is usually expressed through a policy, although in some businesses an executive letter would do. (Experience suggests that a policy is better; it provides a permanence not found in letters, which tend to be forgotten.)

Top management must become aware of the importance of information in the business. The preparation for an information-valuation program should provide an excellent framework for making management aware. The policy proposal should demonstrate the rationale for identifying the various information value levels. Usually, based on governmental practice, these value levels are called classifications. Information that has been assigned a value level is said to be "classified." We will use those terms. To avoid confusion with classified government information, the business' name should always be used in conjunction with the term: "IBM classified" or "Xerox classified." The term *classified* alone usually means government-classified information.

The kind of business one is in determines the number of classifications needed in information valuation. Generally, the more technical a business, the more levels of classification needed. High-technology businesses have many specialized types of information that require valuation.

Remember that the information classification is not protection, per se. The classification results from decisions about information values and is used as a rule to guide security managers (and all employees) in protecting information. Classification is important because we cannot provide effec-

Table 6.1 Relative Information Values and Controls

Valuation level (relative)	Typical title	Restrictions
Highest	Registered	Control use by employee name
High technical	Proprietary	Control by job class
Moderate	Business confidential	Need to know basis—no formal control
Privacy	Personal	Privacy—related Subject and supervisor/staff
Low value	—	All other—private to company; no formal control

tive, practical protection for everything; by identifying high-value information elements we focus the security effort appropriately to the business situation, thereby saving time and money.

Valuation Policy

The policy concerning information classification should explain management's reasoning behind the values categories. The fewer the classifications, the better. Complicated systems of information classification tend to be misunderstood or disregarded. As noted above, there is no specific guideline on how many classifications are needed. But based on the practice of successful companies, from two to four classifications are the rule. Table 6.1 suggests some of the generic classifications used in large businesses.

For each classification, a set of protection criteria must be established. From the restrictions descriptions in Table 6.1 one can readily imagine the kinds of controls appropriate for all forms of business information (mental, written, electronic) having that value level or classification (also see again Figure 4.1). An example of an information valuation schedule, which could be used to obtain management approval for a policy statement, is provided in Appendix III. A policy covering information classification is suggested in Appendix II.

Implementing Information Valuation

It is one thing to set a policy for making information value decisions. It is quite another to ensure (1) that it is done on an initial and continuing basis, and (2) that decisions are made consistent with management's intent and risk posture. This requires crisp, clear definition, motivation, and training. An immediate question is "Who will make classification determinations?" Logically, the assignment of a particular business-information element to a value classification should be made by the information resource manager. But for many companies this may prove awkward; in such cases the data owner or the manager responsible for the primary function generating the data should make immediate classification decisions.

Individual employees may generate innovative information in the course of using personal computers or in their jobs in engineering or research. In these cases, security for this information must depend upon the employee having the know-how and motivation to make a classification decision, apply necessary labels, and take appropriate protection measures. So after the policy is promulgated, providing a basis and authority for information value classification, we must have procedures and practices. These latter directives, called standards, will ensure continuing, reliable decisions about all new information and continuing protection for all information already classified. In sequence, the steps in establishing a business-information valuation process are:

1. Management concept approval
   Information resource value concept
   Classifications matrix
   Exemplary info elements assignment
2. Policy publication
   Definitions of classification
   Authority assignment
   Protection decision rules
3. Standards publication
   Practices
   General classifications guidelines
   General protection requirements for each classification
4. Training meetings and so on

The final purpose of the standards publication is to disseminate throughout the business knowledge of protection requirements. The standards should therefore provide an explanation of the cursory requirements set forth in the policy. This explanation should address, in practical terms, information protection requirements flowing from management's expressed or implied risk-taking posture. (We discuss the matter of risk in Chapter 7.)

The standards should establish clear decision rules about the protection steps necessary once a classification decision has been made. In a high-technology business, these decision rules may be very restrictive at the high-value classification level. In a less exotic business such as a grocery or hardware chain, the few classification levels may require only moderate security effort.

In a practical sense, day-to-day decisions about information classification are made on an objective basis. That is, the manager responsible for the decision must take into consideration a set of circumstantial and fixed rules including:

Business operations environment

Importance of information on competitive posture

Legal requirements

Company policy for specified information elements

Employee, supplier, and public privacy needs.

Of course, certain business-information elements may be obvious candidates for a classification based on subjective decisions; customer and sales files are examples. However, the classification policy (or at least the standard) usually specifies those information elements for which the classification decisions are subjective. This is so because management will try to limit subsequent judgmental decisions on data that is of obvious value.

The business information resource manager should be the source of advice and assistance in making classification decisions. Certainly the security manager should also be knowledgeable and helpful, but the functional managers—the data owners—have the primary responsibility.

Cases

Classifying decisions may be made in many ways and under widely varying circumstances. We can propose a set of such circumstances:

1. The basis for valuation and assignment of a classification is a business policy that establishes the value levels, classification nomenclature, and protection requirement for each.
2. Classification decisions are made formally by the information resource manager, by data owners, or by individual employee information users/ developers.
3. Formal information value decisions are almost always based on objective criteria: the value of the information to the business given the management's risk-taking posture. However, certain information values always result from formal subjective decisions; personnel and medical records, for example, which have a value because of the need for privacy.
4. Informal, on-the-spot decisions, usually but not always objective, are made by employees to provide interim protection until a formal decision can be obtained.

A few examples will help clarify the process:

John A works in a chemistry laboratory. He is aware that certain new product potentials are of great importance to his employer. John also is aware that his company has an information-protection program; however, the experiments he is conducting are in the realm of pure science and have not been classified. One day, John makes a startling discovery. He realizes that he has discovered something that may be of immense value in product terms. He takes upon himself the responsibility to place a classification on the information. He appropriately marks the reports he sends to his superiors. This is a key decision and illustrates a most essential point. All employees must recognize information values and must be trained and motivated to take appropriate steps whenever necessary to maintain the business' rights. John's decision about the value of his discovery may later be modified or even canceled by the responsible information "owner." But he took the correct action in his circumstance, and acted as a responsible employee.

Paul T works for a large oil company as a chemical process engineer and is preparing a report on a new process. When he completes his first draft, he obtains the company's security standards and looks to see if a formal decision has been made on classification for processes. He finds that the type of report he is preparing is identified as "Business Confidential," a medium value level. Paul follows the policy instruction on marking, storing, and restricting distribution. He also instructs his secretary to mark and store the floppy disks from the word processor in the correct manner. Paul T is essentially following instructions prepared by the business information manager or other equivalent authority, expressed through policy and standards. Before he can do so, he must know about the company's information-security program and understand how it relates to him. Continued publicity, training, and motivation efforts have paid off in this case.

David W is an industrial designer who has received a document outlining the design criteria for a new product. He is concerned because the document is being distributed to an unrestricted list, without any indication of classification. David calls his organizational security coordinator, who comes to his office and looks at the document. The security coordinator agrees that the document is of sufficient business value to justify classification; he calls the security coordinator from the originating organization. A decision to classify the document is made by the proper executive. All documents are recalled; proper protection measures are applied. In this case, the secret may already be out. Copies are easy to make. But one alert employee may have saved the day by calling attention to an apparent oversight by the originator of a sensitive document.

Chris A is a systems analyst. Chris knows that the requirements for system development, in his company, require that information security be addressed in early phases of development work. Chris asks the information owner—the system functional user—about the valuation of the information to be processed. This is an important input to decisions on how information will be processed, reports controlled, and the like. The information owner obtains decisions on information classification. Chris can now proceed with systems design. The resulting system should protect the information in line with its business value and management's risk-taking practices, as expressed in policy statements. If the information is typical of that found in most information systems, the decision on classification was based on existing formal value assignments; customer account information, for instance, is classified as XYZ Company Private.

Marybeth S is an executive of a health care company. She must determine the value of information to be held in a customer accounts file. Marybeth uses a set of decision rules. Although she may not recognize the sources, these decision rules come from (1) her knowledge of the health care industry, (2) her awareness of privacy requirements, and (3) her reference to a company policy that spells out practices concerning information valuation and protection. In this case, a category of value seems to fit well, a classification called Customer/Patient Data. This category has an established protection requirement set. Marybeth selects this classification as meeting the needs of this case, in line with management practice and stated policy.

Danny J, generating reports on market penetration for a new product, is using his personal computer. He knows that all market reports are to be classified Private. Danny uses the corporate policy as a reference to make sure that the markings on the reports and the distribution meet security requirements. His training and effort make sure that the marketing reports he produces will have classification and thus protection. These will be equivalent to that provided for the marketing reports generated at the central computer sites in his company.

The Security Function Within IRM

We have seen several different situations in which information valuation was important to protecting the business information resource. And we have seen how proper management decisions, expressed through policy and promulgated through awareness training, allowed good employees to protect information. Classification signals the need for protection; since we can't protect everything, without classification protection won't happen. The framework for this protection is a structure of directives and organization based on the information management principles we have outlined.

Table 6.2 Framework of Directives for Information Security

Policy	General and critical rules
:	
:	
:	
Standards	Practices ensuring consistency of operation across units and locations
:	
:	
:	
Procedures	Local or unit procedures as needed

The overall directives structure for a business information security program can consist of three levels. These are the policy, or general underlying management statement; the standards, the "glue" of the program that provides procedural statements to ensure consistent protection for business information throughout the company; and procedures where needed for local operating convenience. Table 6.2 shows the framework of directives.

The information-security step following information valuation is *policy publication*. The policy is a brief statement of minimums and mandatory requirements. The policy statement will stipulate the levels of information classification (usually not more than four or five) and will provide names for these levels (Registered, Business Confidential, and so on). The policy will also offer broad rules for assigning information elements to value classifications, for example "Information that, if exposed, might seriously damage product development programs is to be classified as Registered."

The policy should address all management concerns with protection of the business information resource. In a large company, this policy might be a part of a broader directive addressing information resource management. The policy should cover the types of valuable information and who may approve release of such information. The general counsel of the business usually has a role when copyrights, trade secrets, or patents must be protected.

When writing policy one may consider that information is of value when these criteria apply:

1. The information is not public, nor is it available from general public sources, such as libraries.
2. It has value to the business and could have value to outsiders; that is, it may provide a competitive difference if one knows or does not know.
3. It is not published within the business in generally distributed booklets, manuals, flyers, policies, standards, and the like that are not controlled.

Getting the policy and the concepts it embodies sold to top management is probably the most essential step in the entire process; without management support at all levels, the program will wither away. A "cascade" announcement is a good way to start out; in this method, the president of the company briefs his or her direct reports on program basics. Each in turn then briefs the next level down, through the entire business.

Once the policy is announced, or concurrent with that announcement, standards development should begin. This step establishes the security-element assignments appropriate to each information classification. That is, each classification indicates a value assigned to an information item; the standard specifies the effort to be expended for each classification. Standards are the cohesive element that holds the program together across various divisions or groups. In smaller businesses, standards can be incorporated into the policy; nevertheless, the specification of actions to be taken in business operations is not policy and will be referred to here as standards. Keep in mind that your particular standards should reflect the minimum requirements for protecting and controlling your information resources. A simple information security process, well understood by all, is always better than a complex, unnecessarily burdensome system.

Following policy announcements comes *publication of standards*, the administrative action elements. The assignment of a number of employees who are knowledgeable about records management, information processing, functional activities, and audit, from across the organization, would be helpful in the development and writing of the directives.

Recognizing of the levels of security elements facilitates development of the standards because we can "mix and match" security-element requirements to tailor solutions to business circumstances. Consider these examples:

● When sensitive business information is to be accessed from a terminal, logical access management (software control) is usually required. But suppose there are only two employees who will use this information and that each has a key to the locked room where the only terminal connected to the files is kept. Then we could simply use physical security—the locked door—and save the cost of the logical security software.

● If a number of clerical employees use computer terminals to enter orders, we may wish to control the process; that is, we want to fix responsibility for the work done. We have several alternatives, among which are

1. Install locking power supplies on each terminal and provide each employee with a unique key. Assuming that the central processor could recognize individual terminals, the keys would do the job of fixing responsibility for us.
2. Install logical access controls in the central computer, assigning each employee a unique password, which would have to be entered before the day's work began. The result would be the same as in 1. Thus we have a flexibility in tailoring an information security effort to our particular business needs.

Table 6.3 Bases for Value Decisions and IRM Actions

Information value decisions	IRM actions

Damage to business from
  Destruction
  Exposure
  Unauthorized change
  Loss
	Classification with appropriate security
	  measures

Damage to business from
  Denial of access
  Unavailability
	Contingency planning

Damage to business from loss of personal privacy	Classification Limited use
Potential liability from exposure or loss	Records management
Potential cost of regeneration or replacement	Seldom used—difficult to measure

There are four basic elements useful to someone wishing to commit fraud using a computer: the business data files, the computer programs used to process those files, the computer or communications system, and access to assets. If any one employee can gain control over two or more of these elements, there is a significant risk. The standard should establish security measures and controls that will fix individual responsibility and limit the potential for any one person to gain enough control to bypass the normal supervisory and audit check points.

The standard should explain the required marking and handling processes for each classification. (Appendix IV provides an example of such a standard.) In setting up an information-security program, remember that most information leaks in today's business occur through the use of printed or written information; pieces of paper are still the favorite way to transfer information to unauthorized persons. Your standard should emphasize the requirements for marking and handling pieces of paper, according to the information values or classifications assigned. We can propose matching value decisions and IRM actions that illustrate the importance of information valuation, as shown in Table 6.3.

The Information Security Network

Information has some characteristics that are unique among business resources. Information occurs in several forms; in electronic form it may have little spatial or time constraints, can be transferred very rapidly, occurs almost everywhere in the business, and is personal to every employee. So we need a special kind of organization for information security. This we

call the information security network. The network means that we want
to get as many employees as possible involved in the business information-
security effort. We will do this by identifying employees at all levels of our
business as information security coordinators, monitors, or whatever name
is appropriate.

Although the use of a network of security coordinators has a straightforward objective of supporting the information resource conservation program, there is an important secondary effect. That effect is the general
distribution, understanding, and acceptance of personal responsibility for
protecting information. This is crucial as most businesses move toward the
personalization of computing, or personal workstation automation. In brief,
most traditional security measures become irrelevant when employees work
at home or in airplanes or hotels and can access business information
resources using terminal devices. In this situation, personal awareness and
acceptance of responsibility is the key.

The information security coordinator (ISC) is an employee not from
security or IRM functions who has been assigned incremental responsibility
to take special efforts to look after the protection of company information
within his or her department, division, or group. Consider these suggested
task characteristics:

1. The information security coordinator may be at any organizational level.
   In some cases, executive ISCs are used.
2. The portion of job working time absorbed by security responsibilities
   ranges from 3 to 20 percent, depending on the type of organization and
   the individuals' other assignments (an administrative aide may have a
   higher proportion than an assembly-line supervisor).
3. Information security coordinators are the primary information security
   resource for line management. The ISC performs a number of important
   functions in maintaining and operating the information security portion
   of the information resource management responsibility. These ISC activities include keeping abreast of developments in company policy and
   standards regarding information security and advising managers and
   training all employees in the group, division, office, and so forth on
   information security practices.
4. The ISC should maintain liaison with the security function and with
   other appropriate activities within his or her department, division, or
   group; as an example, systems development activities should have recourse to information security specialists during project development.

The use of information security coordinators can provide for the development of an increasing cadre of people knowledgeable and concerned
with information management. As ISCs are replaced or as ISC duties are
rotated, numbers of employees are exposed to the rationale and details of
the program. Over a period of years the company develops a general

employee capability and awareness for conserving the critical business information resource. This is no small advantage in a competitive and constraint-free age.

An initial assignment of a number of key people as information security coordinators can be of help in the formative stages of your program. These people, from all parts of the company, can assist the information resource manager and security manager in developing a practical program. These assignments should be made immediately after the publication of the policy.

In summary, the initial stages of your program consist of these actions, in sequence:

1. Develop management awareness and risk position regarding business information.
2. Develop and publish policy concerning business information values, related classification terminology, and important information-use restrictions to be broadly applied across the business.
3. Appoint an initial set of information security coordinators from all company functions to aid in developing information security standards.
4. Begin process of identifying and classifying valuable business information elements.
5. Publish information security standards.
6. Appoint and train appropriate additional information security coordinators to ensure adequate support across the organization.
7. Initiate audit program activity.

Factors for Success and Failure

Many business programs intended to conserve the business information resource fail to do the job. Professionals tell of their frustrations with weak management support, confusing and incomplete efforts, and lack of understanding about intentions and methods. Why is this so, and how can we best avoid these problems?

Let us begin by proposing a definition of an effective information resource management system. This is not a perfect definition; the business environment, objectives, and risk-acceptance posture of your business will shape your definition. You should have your own custom-made definition clearly in mind before you begin structuring and implementing your own program.

Our basic definition: An *effective information resource program* is one that manages the business information resource so as to ensure information integrity, reliability, and control. The program is based upon management recognition of information values, expressed through classification. Management control over the business information resource is accomplished by means of information use authorizations that establish individual user responsibility. Such responsibility is fixed through the application of combinations of security elements in a manner and at a cost appropriate to established information resource values and business requirements. You may of course change that definition as you desire, but it does give us a fairly good target for our program. Notice that there are a number of subsidiary targets within the definition, including:

1. To identify high-value information so that we expend our scarce (expensive) control efforts on the proper information elements. The valuing of information can be done either subjectively or objectively, as described in Chapter 2.
2. To establish individual user responsibility. This is in line with normal business practice in using other resources. Budget managers authorize expenditures. Supplies managers authorize issuances from storerooms. The information resource manager should authorize the use of the information asset. Of course, we may not precisely control low-level items such as pencils and the same rule may apply to low-value information; it may not be controlled at all in some businesses.
3. To fit the cost and selection of security elements to the particular operating needs of the business. In other words, the program we develop should be appropriate to the requirements and capabilities of our company. We should be thinking like business managers as we build the program, keeping in mind the risk-taking position of our top management. We may, of course, have to ask them what this risk assumption should be.
4. The security elements we implement should be applied according to the established information values in our business. We should have a clear understanding of the most critical, highest-value information so that we can address attention to providing really robust security for this information. Probably, if your business is like most, you'll find that you are really worried about only 1 percent or so of the total information resource. That is usually the portion of the information resource which would seriously affect the business operation and profits if compromised or destroyed.
5. We are trying to provide information integrity and reliability and control by this security program. Security elements and their proper application are means to a business end. Successful operation requires that our company have information with the qualities of integrity, reliability, and control. Security does not of itself provide these qualities; employee supervision, systems design, and training are also needed. Also, security does not ensure continuity of operation. Contingency planning, a general management responsibility, must address the concern for continuing business viability should a disaster occur. So our definition tells us precisely in which responsibility area we operate; this is important if we

are to build an effective program. One cannot do a good job if responsibilities are not clearly defined and limited. Our responsibilities, then, under the proposed definition are to design and apply security elements to provide protection commensurate with information values. And we must do this at a cost and in a manner appropriate to our company's mode of operations and risk-assumption practices.

6. To fix responsibilities, the combination of security elements should provide means to monitor what is happening, especially with regard to high-value information. In certain cases, the monitor system should provide precise event or transaction records (as now required for personnel records in some European countries or as most managers would require for cash-transfer operations). Other situations may require only that a general activity trace allow for after-the-fact audit capabilities.

We have proposed a set of guidelines for getting the program started successfully. Now, let's consider what causes programs to fail; then perhaps we can avoid those problems. After looking at what went wrong, we can develop a what-to-do list to ensure a reasonably effective information-protection program.

According to James S. Moyer, an information management consultant in Westminster, California (Moyer, 1983), information programs will not succeed unless a senior executive has responsibility for total information resource management. And Arnold Miller (1983) says that poor management understanding, lack of a plan, and weak management commitment to information management result in ineffectual attempts at control. At a large New York corporate headquarters attempts to install an information protection program have been only partially successful because the controls were limited to computer-output information; the company has not seen information in all forms as a valuable asset. Management responsibilities are so fragmented at a company in Connecticut that it is not clear who is responsible for information resource control. Various staff groups went different ways, resulting in confusion at working levels and inconsistency in handling various forms of information. Value judgments are not consistent and rules for handling differ for the different forms of information for the same information item. A California business lost some of its competitive advantage when employees "gave away" proprietary information through a series of blunders. The compromise occurred because the company had failed to establish an authority to control information. In the management vacuum that existed, confusing signals from various managers resulted in a loss of control.

Planning for Effective Information Protection

Let's now review some requirements in light of the faults we have just seen, and with our proposed definition as a guide.

1. Have clear and unambiguous top-management understanding and support for information resource management concepts. This should include an understanding of the role of security in helping ensure economy of use, integrity, availability, and control.
2. Make sure the program concepts for your business mesh well with your management's risk-acceptance posture. Your program must fit your business needs in terms of protection and cost.
3. Establish information-value decisions, resulting in classifications, for the principal business-information elements of your company. These classifications must be suitable to business requirement; the tail must never wag the dog. Avoid overvaluing and overclassification. Apply protection elements in combinations and at costs appropriate to information values.
4. Make sure information protection applies across all forms. This means telling employees what they may talk about: Eastman Kodak Company in Rochester, New York, has done an outstanding job of motivating employees to be tight-lipped. Information security has become a part of the employee culture at Kodak. This has resulted from years of consistent training and discipline based on effective policies and programs. Rules and handling procedures must ensure a continuity and consistency of protection across all information forms. Avoid going overboard on electronic forms.
5. Establish clear responsibility for valuing (classifying) information, and make sure that employees understand what to do if they generate novel information requiring a decision. Take necessary actions within the business environment of your company to motivate employees. Provide training so that people know what an information-classification indicator means in terms of information care and protection.
6. Emphasize the business-related aspects of information security. Keep repeating the need for the protection effort to be in harmony with business operations. Explain the risks to business viability and profitability if valuable information resources are squandered.
7. Establish effective controls over information-processing activities, including manual processes. Controls include good supervision, separation of duties, audit trails, checkpoints, and the like. Build information management concepts into the information systems development process; valuation and information-resource use authorizations should be a part of the early design phases of system development. This is true whether managed formally in a large company or informally in smaller businesses.

(The Appendixes provide a wealth of information and references for the manager anxious to "get started.")

III | Practical Business Decisions

7 | Making Effective Security Decisions Within the Information Management Function

In planning for the expenditure of resources on information security, business managers select investments based upon some rational criteria. Among the decision elements are information values, both objective and subjective (see Chapter 5), and risk. Risk refers to the circumstances and conditions surrounding business operations. Unfavorable circumstances and conditions make up the risk element in a business decision. These circumstances may be evident, or they may be projections based on the manager's best information.

Risks are either current or potential. *Current risks* are evident and continuing and typically result from the operating environment. They include such things as the danger of explosion if powders are processed and dangers from location in a neighborhood prone to crime, arson, or riot; current risks are inherent to a business operation, location, or process. The use of extensive information systems networks and local processors constitutes current risk (for errors, possible misrouting of data, system failures, and so on), but one most modern businesses accept as a part of doing business. It is very difficult to imagine a business with no current risks. Designing a security system to protect against current risks is not terribly difficult, however, as the risk is identifiable and the solution fairly obvious.

Potential risk, which may result from some indeterminate action, intentional or unintentional, is outside the normal and purposeful business operation. Potential risks include penetrations into supposedly private computer files, fires, break-ins, theft of information, and wiretapping. Managers worry most about potential risks. We would like to have assurances that our information resource is protected against the most serious and most likely attacks. (Errors are an IRM issue, not an information security issue; they have to do with information integrity. The elimination or control of errors is a general management responsibility addressed through training, supervision, and systems design.)

Probability theory can be used to determine the likelihood of an event occurring if sufficient historical data are available. In the insurance industry, premiums are based on such collections of actual incident data as mortality tables. These data allow the insurance industry to make accurate projections of the average age expectancy, average frequency of accidents, and the like for a given group of policyholders with similar characteristics. The insurance manager can then be reasonably certain that premiums will, over time, cover policy payments. The efficiency of this method lies in the large amounts of data in the population: A sample of two people would not give much information of value as to the likelihood of one of them dying, but two million cases would provide accurate statistical information, allowing accurate development of probability.

The business manager concerned with providing security for the information resource would like to have the same degree of surety as the insurance manager. We would like to be able to say to management that the probability of such-and-such happening is X, the value to the business is Y, and that as a result we propose to spend Z dollars on protection.

Business is, after all, the taking of risk. Top executives got to their coveted jobs by evaluating situations and then making calculated decisions to take risks. If they were right, large profits resulted, but management literature is full of cases where the gamble failed. The lesson is obvious; the people to whom the security function reports, and for whom any security program is designed, are risk-takers. A program for the identification and protection of the business resource called information must take into account this important fact. A simple formula approach won't work, because top management will not accept it and will not support it. Like other parts of the business process, the security measures within an information resource management program must be practical, flexible, and in tune with business needs. Table 7.1 illustrates management responses to various information vulnerabilities.

The information protection effort must be based on a *business approach* that recognizes alternatives and decision choices at each step. To understand this concept we will consider the risk-management function in most businesses, which generally has to do with providing insurance coverage. But any risk management has a decision format of value to us for information management and protection purposes.

Risk Management

Risk managers view the business and all its resources as values requiring some assurance of continuity and recoverability. In making selections among measures to provide assurances, these alternatives are considered:

1. Accept risk as a part of doing business: Bringing out a new product is almost always such a risk acceptance. If the product fails, the loss must be absorbed by other revenue streams. Self-insurance, common in large businesses, is a form of risk acceptance.
2. Make changes in the mode of operations to avoid a risk. An example of such a management decision is a switch to a dealership distribution network, rather than direct sales, for a new product. The dealer network then absorbs some of the risk in carrying inventory. Another example is a change to a different manufacturing process when the original method is found to generate toxic materials.
3. A portion of the risk associated with an operation can be transferred to others through insurance.
4. Risks can be controlled and limited through the use of various protective measures, the option we call *security* in most businesses. Note that we say risks can be "controlled and limited," not eliminated. Whatever information-resource program we recommend must be attuned to our management's chosen risk-taking position. Management must recognize that there is no risk-free business-information environment.

A reasonable and practical information-protection program in the information age must be in tune with the business process. A program that responds only to threats of "computer crime" will be inappropriate because it will be out of tune with the process of running the overall business. The risk-management approach offers a way to develop a program that will mesh with ongoing business management practices. Being in line with top management's views of business, it will be supported and thus provide continuity and currency of protection. Risk decisions may be envisioned as a set of decisions and actions:

Decision	Action
Avoid risk	Change mode of operation
Control risk	Implement management controls and protections (IRM)
Limit risk	Procure insurance coverage
Accept risk	Proceed as planned

Most business managers choose a combination of actions from the alternatives.

Risk options for the manager developing an information-protection scheme flow from the directives structure and from decisions concerning information valuation (Chapter 6). Management decides to accept ever-greater risks in the use of the information resource as the definitions of protected classes of information are narrowed. In some businesses, a rational decision may be made to protect only one or two data elements from

Table 7.1 Information Vulnerabilities and Management Actions

Information vulnerabilities			Management actions		
				Information valuation decision	
Vulnerability	Source	Cause	Written form	Electronic form	Mental form
Exposure to unauthorized parties	Inside	Carelessness	Procedure Supervision	Logical control Training	Motivation
		Intentional	Motivation Supervision	Motivation Logical control	Contract
	Outside	Industrial espionage	Physical control	Logical control	N/A
		Other	Physical control	Logical control	N/A
Damage to information Base records/files	Inside	Carelessness	Supervision Procedure	System procedure Supervision	N/A
		Intentional	Motivation Procedure/control	Logical control	N/A
	Outside	Industrial espionage	Physical control	Logical control	N/A
		Other	Physical control	Logical control	N/A
Loss of information Base records/files	Inside	Destruction due to carelessness	Supervision Procedure	System procedure Back-up files	N/A
		Disaster	Contingency plan	Contingency plan	Travel restriction

			Back-up files	Back-up files	Policy
High-value business information	Outside	Destruction due to attack	Physical control Back-up files Contingency plan Back-up files	Logical control Back-up files Contingency plan Back-up files	N/A
		Disaster			N/A
Loss of Information—legal requirement	Inside	Destruction	Physical control Vault storage Procedure	System procedure Vault storage Procedure	N/A
		Loss (mis-placement)			N/A
Loss of reliability (destruction or impairment of infrastructure)	Inside	System failure	N/A	Fault tolerant system System recovery plan Contingency plan Back-up files	N/A
		Disaster	Back-up files Contingency plan		N/A
	Outside	Attack	Physical control Contingency plan	Logical control Physical control Contingency plan	N/A
		Disaster (including secondary cause, e.g., nuclear emission)			N/A

the total information resource. In other, high-technology businesses the protective measures must address almost all business information. The proportion of the total information resource contained within the value classifications in large extent determines the cost of the protection effort.

The decision to accept risk must be made in line with the overall IRM structure and is not a decision to be made in isolation. As information-value decisions increase the scope and/or valuation of information in protected groups, security costs go up; if the program is well constructed, risks should decrease at the same time, thus constraining management-accepted risks in using these high-value information elements.

Risk Analysis

Managers like to support decisions with analytical data. We can estimate risks by developing probability estimates and projecting these against values set in the information classification process. This approach is *Risk analysis*, a popular and often-proposed method to arrive at some degree of certainty. In *Managing Information Security: A Program for the Electronic Information Age* (1982) I discuss the features and flaws in risk analysis as currently practiced. Here we need only note that present versions of the risk-analysis method, as applied to making decisions on security of information, do not generate data of a quality that would be acceptable for other management decisions of equal importance. This happens because the methods generally offered use a formula that multiplies order-of-magnitude estimates of cost by statistically unsupported estimates of probability. The results of such computations are suspect because of the absence of reliable inputs: too many of the data used are the results of generalizations. If management is willing to accept a "guestimate" as support for a decision, risk analysis will provide it.

Practitioners of the method, which typically takes the form of costly committee projects or software investments, retort that the results of their work are "better than nothing." They are also much more expensive than nothing, and there are alternative ways to ensure that information security is tuned to the business' needs.

Risk analysis is nevertheless valuable in certain very constrained circumstances, among which are:

1. Where a business has established information security requirements and, because of operating circumstances, responsible information managers determine that it is preferable to take a risk than to bear the costs associated with the policy compliance. In this case risk analysis provides data that may assist management in making a valid decision to accept an element of risk. The risk analysis is performed on only one situation or system; there is no attempt to portray the results as a guide to setting up a security program.

2. Given an established business operation with security elements in place, management wishes to ascertain if unusual risk is being incurred. An example would be a risk analysis of a cash-transfer system in a large corporation. Such an analysis would help management understand the types and probabilities associated with high-value cash transfers. The analysis would not be used as the basis for design of security measures, some of which are already in place. It might identify additional protection needed.

Among the serious potential problems of risk analysis is the possibility of overlooking an exposure while assuring management that everything is covered. Security elements should not be applied like bandages, stuck wherever the risk analysis shows a potential concern. Seldom if ever do frauds or other information misuses occur in expected places or ways.

In sum, the information output of a typical security risk analysis varies in quality. The probability estimates may be slightly more reliable than the cost exposure estimates; both are often seriously suspect because of the absence of valid historical data. Risk analysis may be of relative value in limited instances, but only as a decision help when other criteria are in place.

The IRM Alternative

Consider the average householder in a large city. The possibility of burglary is usually obvious. The householder determines the actual or sentimental value of possessions and then goes about making somewhat rational decisions about protection. Among those decisions may be:

Placing high-value portable items (jewelry, negotiable instruments, important papers) in a safe-deposit box.

Installing a home burglar alarm system.

Placing stronger or additional locks on doors and windows.

Instructing the family in good security practices.

Installing additional outside lighting.

These decisions are made based on the owner's sense of inherent values in people and things. They are also based on the ability to pay for the security features. The final decisions almost always reflect the householder's willingness to bear risk.

An information-security program can be based on the same kind of judgments. The information resource manager makes the decisions about the business values of various information types. Appropriate security elements are then applied to provide the general level of security for each valuation (in this case, information classification). Using information values as the basis for security planning is consistent with other security management:

1. Security protection should be consistent with the value of the item being protected.
2. Security protection should remain with the valuable item at all times as it is moved or processed.
3. Security protection should be continuous in all situations.

A risk analysis may identify several high-risk situations and security efforts are therefore directed toward them. But information is not static; it moves about as the business operates. The attack may occur at places or in situations unforeseen. The protection must therefore be consistent, always in effect. Using information value as the basis for protection is also more consistent with the traditional management approach to other problems that are difficult to quantify. The data generated by a risk-analysis method would probably not be acceptable to financial managers as a basis for an investment decision; yet if risk analysis is used to determine security spending, we are doing just that.

If information is the critical resource for business, our method should reflect the concept that information is what is being protected, not computers or facilities. Security structures should be designed for—and applied to—information elements according to their business value or classification. The selection of security elements is based on classification; the information security standards (see Chapter 6 and Appendix IV) specify which levels of security elements apply to various classifications of information and to special situations.

Security Levels and Elements

An IRM program must address various information-control, -utilization, and -protection issues. Protection of the information resource depends on the proper and reasonable application of security measures. To help us envision this application, consider the security measures as being in three *levels*. Within each level we have a set of security *elements*, the basic security building blocks. These levels and their constituent elements are:

1. *Physical* measures—those controlling physical access to information such as door locks, guards, video monitors, desk locks, safes; provision of restricted areas, card-controlled doors, identification badges.
2. *Procedural* measures—those administrative tasks required to maintain control over information. These might include the marking and special handling of documents, records of people entering a restricted area, records of the distribution and receipt of high-value documents, records of computer accesses printed out by the computer system and reviewed by security people, authorization lists created and maintained by a systems administrator showing what information uses are approved for

individual systems users, personnel administration processes that cause cancellation or change of access authorities when employees have job changes or leave the company's employ, and so on. Procedural security elements often involve the investigation of potential employees being considered for sensitive positions. This may require a credit check, interviewing of friends or past employers, and verifying educational qualifications. For most jobs, this is a practical approach. Unfortunately, for people who are to be involved in high-technology work, history casts doubt on this effort. The typical "computer miscreant" has had the highest credentials, a model employee and an excellent worker. This reinforces the need for good hiring practices, which should always include contractual arrangements (nondisclosure agreements) to protect the business' right to its proprietary information (Spanner, 1984).

3. *Logical* security measures—which include the software programs and hardware features and functions providing controls over who uses computer resources and what these authorized users may do. Logical security elements also maintain records of system events; these records almost always interface with procedural security elements, which allow for human inspection and monitoring of the logical records. An example of a logical measure is a program that allows a user to sign on and then requires that he or she enter an identifying password before allowing processing to take place. The potential logical security controls using software constructions are almost limitless, constrained only by cost of operation. A special type of logical security element is called *encryption*, the encoding or masking of information through the use of a complex algorithm that converts an intelligent information stream (clear text) into a nonrepetitive substitution character stream (encrypted). Such an encoded stream of information is virtually undecipherable, even by experts with computers, unless one has the code key. Because the encryption logical security element is so robust, it will eventually be the primary security protection for all high-value information.

By selecting a mix of security elements from the appropriate levels for a given information value or for a given circumstance of business operation, an effective and reasonable security protection standard can be established. *Reasonable* means that it will be in line with management's determined risk posture; this may be different from the protection levels desired by the security manager, who may have a "100-percent positive" security viewpoint. In other words, security professionals often do not want to take risks, while business managers see risk-taking as part of the game.

Considering the many security elements within the three levels of security measures the ingredients of a recipe to suit the taste of management for risk-taking is useful. Figure 7.1 shows such a recipe, the selection process of choosing various security elements to meet a vulnerability. The information resource manager has specified the information values and restric-

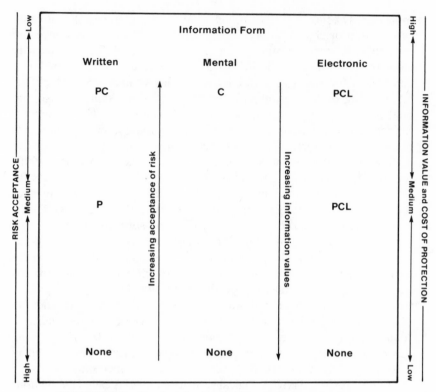

ELEMENTS: P = Physical L = Logical C = Procedural/Contractual

Figure 7.1 Selection of security elements to meet a given information value and
           risk acceptance.

tions, based on management decisions values about information value and
risk-taking. The security manager must create a suitable protective mix of
the security elements to meet management's published (policy) or implied
(business practice) risk acceptance/security needs. (Application of the security elements is discussed later in this chapter.)

Meeting Business Needs

A most important step in the process of developing computer systems
applications is analyzing the user's requirements. Properly done, this analysis should result in the development of a systems specifications document
that describes clearly what the computer system is supposed to do. Unfortunately, however, systems analysts are infamous for developing systems
that do not meet the user's needs. Usually this has happened because the
analyst did not—or would not—understand what the user's problem really

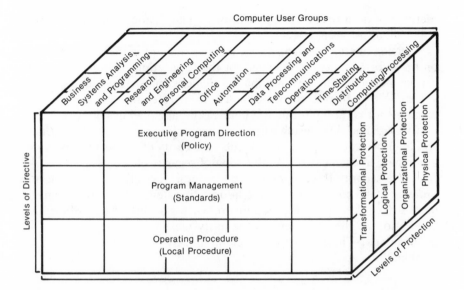

Figure 7.2 Program structure, three-dimensional matrix. *(Source:* J.A. Schweitzer, *Managing Information Security – A Program for the Electronic Information Age* (Woburn, Mass., 1982), reprinted with permission of Butterworth Publishers.)

was. The system, then, was designed to satisfy the analyst's cravings for technical perfection. Users ended up with information systems that were beautiful in concept but failed to solve their business problems.

Security experts tend to have the same difficulty in dealing with information resource management. Through experience and knowledge of security technology the security manager has an idealized picture of what protection should be. It is much more difficult to "cook up" a recipe of security ingredients that meets management's tastes: the particular style of risk-taking used in a business may not be easy to determine. If the business has formal policies (highly recommended; see Chapter 6), the policy statements are an excellent guide.

Selecting and Applying Security Elements

An effective view of the three-dimensional relationships among security levels, management policy structure, and business applications requiring protection of information is provided in Figure 7.2. This figure is a convenient way to conceptualize the security structure. At each plane within the figure are a number of three-dimensional intersections. Each intersection represents the conjunction of management directives, levels of protection, and information applications. The reader can insert more applications as desired.

Selection of security elements for the intersections in the matrix depends on the information values defined for the applications; within each application, individual files and information elements may have unique specified values. Although one cannot establish fixed rules for selecting security elements for certain information items, general guidelines are possible.

If we assume three established information valuations (high, medium, and low), we can propose assignments of security elements to those value groupings. In each case, a combination of security elements from each of the three security levels (physical, procedural, logical) should result in a protection and cost attuned to the information-item value and to management's risk-taking posture. (See Figure 4.1 for an illustration of element applications.) The three levels of security measures are segregations for convenience. Their constituent elements are almost always used in combination.

Physical Level

Physical security elements make up the oldest and the traditional "industrial security" function. Essentially, this level consists of the many elements that serve to separate the people who are welcome in and around a business activity from those who are not. Joe Rosetti, Security Director for IBM, says that the purpose of security is to "protect and keep what is ours." Physical security elements are almost always used in any circumstance at business locations. However, the distribution of information processing to the personal-services level means that physical security becomes less important in certain applications. It is impractical to devise physical-security-element applications for the manager or professional using a business terminal or microcomputer in a public place or at home. Physical security remains critical for the central information bases, usually in specialized facilities called data centers, which are becoming the information resource storehouses. In fact, the idea of information resource management in the modern age presupposes organized general purpose files; the nature and size of businesses using such general purpose files indicate large file stores. A *file*, as used here, is any collection of business information; a *general purpose file* is one that may be referenced by many different business functions and is usually stored on computer disks. The maintenance, servicing, and connection of multiple functional users to these central files means large file processors. These are the large computers typically found in data centers. So we see that physical security may be supplemented or replaced in distributed applications but remains important for centralized data stores. The typical business office almost always has some physical security elements in operation; this may be only the fact that employees recognize everyone who works there, but there is nevertheless, an effective restraint on outsiders.

Most large businesses establish physical controls over all facilities. This has become more important as cases of attacks by deranged or dissatisfied employees or malevolent outsiders increase. The primary reason for such security is physical protection; nonetheless, the business information usually found in great profusion in offices is an important resource to be protected. For the information resource, then, physical security elements are needed, but almost always in combination with elements from one of the other two levels. And, contrary to protection methods for other business resources—where physical elements remain the principal barrier—physical security is becoming less important as a consideration in information resource management.

Procedural Level

Although the glamour and noise surround the purely logical or electronic threats (the high-tech risks), a very large portion of the problems experienced in the business environment have to do with administrative failures. In the business world of the mid-1980s, procedure is where attention is needed. The vast majority of cases of fraud, theft of information, and other information-related business problems involve the unauthorized use of computing resources, improper entries during change of information form, or through misuse of computer terminals. The most common attacks, of course, are theft of information on pieces of paper. (Certainly some of these may have been printed by a computer printer, but, as we have stated before, that is not a computer-related crime per se.)

Seven years' experience suggest that 95 percent or more of computer misuse in business is the result of failures in procedural security elements. A frequent problem concerns the trusted employee who leaves the company. The administrative process for separation fails to cancel the person's computer-access rights (password), so he or she continues to use the company's computer resources although no longer employed. This use very often takes the form of running a personal business of some kind. Another common occurrence is the use of fraudulent entries to computer files when controls are inadequate or not enforced. Everyday users gain great insight into the workings of computer systems; this often lets them spot inconsistencies or "holes" in the process. If effective audits and supervisory controls have not been provided (a common failing with automated systems) the employee may be tempted to take advantage of the fact. These are the most common forms of computer abuse, and probably the most significant. We don't hear much in the press about the smaller cases because the effects are usually not noticed and the businesses involved, when a case *is* discovered, keep it quiet. Theft of computer services and unauthorized transfers of information are often intangibles, frequently not recognized, and seldom made public. These are usually the result of procedural blunders, not technical cleverness.

Procedural security elements take a wide variety of forms, but most have to do with the control of authorizations to do things and monitoring/auditing those authorized actions after the fact. Procedural security is seldom found to operate without one of the other security levels (physical, logical) because it forms the management-control connection for these other two levels. Some forms of procedural security are:

Maintenance of lists of authorized employees for control of entrance to buildings, issuance of identification cards, authorizations for access to computing resources, use of telecommunications services; records of issuance of account numbers, passwords, or other identification or authentication tokens, and so on.

Processing new employees and separation of terminated employees so that authorizations of special rights and privileges are properly granted and withdrawn. Examples of such privileges include parking for automobiles, controlled-area access badges or codes, keys, passwords, provision of business documents, laboratory notebooks, library items, supplies and equipment needed at work, and tools. It is important that security administrators have a close working relationship with personnel managers to ensure that such personnel actions as separations and reassignments result in the correct security procedures. Where possible (especially where automated systems are in use in personnel and security functions) automated connections between the systems should be set up. (A frequent observation has been the security administrator laboriously key-entering employee data to a security computer when the printout is a personnel report generated from a computer. Absurd!)

Procedure to ensure that departing employees have signed nondisclosure agreements or other contractual documents to safeguard proprietary information. This is especially important in a technology-related business and may be more critical than regaining keys, property, and the like from separating employees.

Office procedures for the marking and handling of documents containing information bearing a value-indication classification. These procedures may include special distribution methods. In some large companies, the highest classifications of documents cannot be removed from company property. If they are needed at another site, a library arranges for a controlled transfer to a library at the site on which they will be used.

Special procedures for marking and control of computer-generated printed documents. These may require printing of special value-related logos, assembly and control before distribution, and receipting on delivery. Some of these procedures, such as for display of information-value logos on video display screens, involve logical elements, described below.

Monitoring logs generated by computer systems that report on employee accesses to buildings, computer systems, and laboratories and may provide indications of improper use or clues to ongoing theft or fraud. This is a common area for the failure of the procedural elements of security. Systems may provide records of what is happening, but in a business environment where manning has been cut to the bone, these logs may go unnoticed. Another important kind of log or record is in the central data center, where the operating system records operator events. Careful examination of these records, which should be maintained on numbered continuous forms or on tapes, can provide an effective audit trail of what happened during computer and network operations.

Supervision and review, and subsequent audit, of transactions processed. Although not security-related, these management responsibilities have a strong bearing on control of business operations. Security problems often result if management fails to provide effectively designed systems, strong controls, good employee training, and proper supervision.

Procedural security elements are essential to information management and control, equal in importance to physical and logical elements. Their locus, in terms of electronic information, is in the access/management systems (described below).

Logical Security

The hardware and software engineering in any computing system provides the opportunity to implement security measures. Properly used, these logical security measures should make information stored or processed on computers *more* secure than information in mental or written form. Unfortunately, the potential power for security protection inherent in software and hardware engineering is more often than not bypassed in favor of economies and processing efficiencies. As usual, everything has its costs, and logical security elements are relatively expensive. We therefore see microcomputers and office systems being produced with little or no effective security built in. The user must do the security job by imaginative, and sometimes unusual constructions of hardware and software barriers.

Logical security elements include data encryption. An encryption system offers the highest efficiency of protection: breaking the code would require a major effort. Information can be encrypted using hardware or software. Encryption is not cheap and is generally used only for the highest value of business information.

The most important forms of logical security have to do with access management systems. Other types of logical security include hardware designs that positively separate users during processing; privileged code that is available only to software maintenance engineers (a group of people who have the keys to your kingdom via the operating system of the computer, whether you like it or not; you should know who they are and how they are managed); data-storage read and write control features; and similar control elements built into the computer system by the manufacturer. Remember that all software, and much hardware, has engineering faults that result in "holes"—which is why there are always people around, expert specialists or amateur hackers, who can find their way through the best security system.

Stories about such people are plentiful in the computer world. Two examples are personal to the author. In case one, a software engineer became an auditor for a large business. He audited a data center and of course was able to break through the logical security system. After writing in the audit report that the security system was defective, he was reminded that there were only two or three people like him in the company. He modified the report, recognizing that with today's level of software perfection, a business just cannot afford "perfect" protection. In a second case, an air force officer responsible for a "tiger team" attempting to break into military systems was having spectacular successes. This officer reported that the most difficult part of the assignment was finding the telephone numbers to call. The conclusion must be that no matter how efficient our logical security constructs, we end up having to trust certain key people.

Access Management

In the electronic information age, for most modern business information resource managers logical security means *access management*. The term refers to the process of implementing and operating and monitoring controls over the use of business computer resources. The users of these resources, from a logical security viewpoint, may be persons or software programs. The latter may access information as part of a retrieval system that polls terminals, asking for data. There are many other applications in business in which programs are users. Access management systems have three essential parts:

1. *Identification*: the claim to be a certain person or program. This claim is supported by the claimant's offer to the system of something the claimant knows, has, or is; this is called a token and can be an identification number or log-on id (most common), a magnetic card, a fingerprint, a voiceprint, a handprint, or the answer to a question.

2. *Authentication*: proof of the identity claim made in the identification step. Preferably, this step will use a token different from that used in the identification step and, to be effective, the token must be secret to the individual user. The access management system should establish positive responsibility of the individual authenticated user for all actions against the computer system, which cannot be done if the authentication token is shared with other users. Passwords are the most common form of token used for authenticating a claimed identity. Unfortunately, passwords have serious weaknesses, including the typical user's propensity for choosing easily guessed passwords, forgetting them, writing them down where others may see them, and sharing them with others. Systems that require issuance of passwords to users are unacceptable because the information resource manager can never pin down a responsibility for improper actions. There are always at least two suspects.

The token must be responsive to the need to fix responsibility for use of the information resource. Recently developed technology offers more effective tokens, such as fingerprint scans, voice-pattern recognition, hand-geometry measurements, and eye-retina scans. These measures provide highly reliable *individual* authentication, which is necessary if we are to ensure real controls over the electronic information resource. These methods are fairly expensive today but should be more reasonably priced as technology becomes cheaper.

3. *Authorization*: the function of the access management system that reflects and enforces the information resource manager's decisions about "who may do what." The authorizations granted to a user must always be specific, never general or "all other." Although authorization is the last step in the access management operational process, it is the first step in implementing an access management system. That is, the information resource manager or data owner must determine those actions needed, via the computer, in the course of business operations. Specific actions must then be authorized to the users. Examples of the authorized actions may be

  Display information only

  Move information to other places or system

  Update information

  Process information against certain programs

  Process information against any program

  Erase or replace information.

An example of an access management system in use may be helpful here. Consider a sales branch in a large company. The branch manager has appointed a security controller, who may authorize various branch employees to access database files on the company's central computer. The security controller has a special authenticator that allows him or her to access the authorization files in the access control system at the central computer.

The sales clerks are authorized, via a branch identifier and a secret personal authentication code, to enter customer orders and to view information on customer orders. Once the clerk has entered the branch identifier and the personal authentication code, the central computer uses the access management system to look up on a magnetic disk a table that indicates the authorized processes for that authentication number. The access management system also makes a record of the access, including date and time. The application system, which is reached through the access management system, may also make a record of the clerk number and keep a log of transaction data. (This is not a part of the security system, however, but an error control process. As mentioned earlier, errors are not a security matter but a concern for supervision, training, and systems design.)

The branch manager is authorized to look at customer account records and to make adjustments thereto. The process is the same.

The branch shipping manager can display unfilled customer orders and can obtain shipping information and instructions. The access process is the same.

At the central computer site a security manager monitors branch security controller activities and provides technical assistance as needed. The data owner or information resource manager provides control and monitoring functions over the accounts and customer activities. Thus the information resource manager ensures that business information is correctly and accurately handled and free from unintentional errors. The security system helps ensure information integrity—and privacy— by restricting access, limiting functionality for any one individual and creating an audit trail that can establish personal responsibility.

Our discussion of the branch office did not address the question of information valuation. Presumably, the information resource manager would already have made decisions about the information values. No doubt customer identification data and credit data would have a value that would justify protection. Also, customer credit data may need to be protected for privacy reasons. The application of a mix or "recipe" of security elements from the three levels should be designed to meet the information valuation, privacy requirements, and the business situation. The latter includes the operating environment: a branch office in a high-risk area where crime is a serious problem would require more elements from the physical level. Too, a properly designed information resource management structure will provide the correct information valuation, or classifications. A good security and access management system will offer the right level of security to protect that information in line with business circumstances and the operating environment. The general rules for application of the security elements should, as always, reflect management's risk-taking posture.

To repeat, the threat of computer-related crime is only peripheral to the decisions about security investment. Essentially, these investment decisions rely upon (1) information values, (2) business operating needs and environment, and (3) practical applications to day-to-day business operating methods.

For some types of information, the ordinary business security may suffice; employee awareness of who should be involved will be all that is necessary. Depending on management's risk-taking philosophy, additional elements from the three levels may be needed, all the way to a full security structure including data encryption:

1. Of course, such facilities as data centers or laboratories require special security attention, and these requirements are different from those of information resources. The difference is in the quality of the vulnerability. Usually a facility vulnerability is a type risk; the facility doesn't move around. Information vulnerabilities are usually potential risks, many of which we do not know about.
2. A risk-analysis approach (as a basis for a program of information security) may result in security measures being installed in static fashion. But the exposures move as the information moves; there is a danger that an important vulnerability will be missed. Using information values as the basis for assigning protective measures provides a consistent protection with the data element, wherever or whenever it appears.
3. Building an information protection program using information values as a basis is consistent with the information resource management concepts so important in business today. It is a modern, information-age approach. The risk-analysis approach views the information processes as fixed elements, much the same as security has traditionally viewed facilities. There is a danger of seeing the computer rather than the information as the critical resource.

Table 7.1 shows how a properly designed and implemented information resource security effort will provide consistent protection for information at all times, in line with management's risk-taking posture and the assigned business information values. Information values, reflected as information classifications, are the basis for the application of security elements. Risk analysis is a supplementary tool for use in specific limited instances where management needs additional data to support unusual decisions or to meet exceptional risk concerns.

8 | Technology and Information Security

In his excellent *Modern Methods for Computer Security and Privacy* (1977) Lance Hoffman provides some security design principles that we will consider before we begin our discussion of technology elements for security:

1. The default is always to a secure situation; that is, if a functional manager fails to specify the classification of data and hence the protection needed, access to that data will be denied in the absence of specific authorization. This is an essential fail-safe principle.
2. The design of the security system is made public and people are asked to comment on it. If a system is not strong or reliable enough to bear scrutiny by friends *and enemies*, it is probably not trustworthy.
3. The security process must not impose an undue burden on the users of the system. If it is either too complex or too time-consuming/costly, *users will find a way to avoid it and security will be compromised.*
4. Every request for access must be validated. Requests from programs must be validated the same as requests from persons. Prior authentications cannot be reused; the system checks authority proof each time access is requested, even for repeated requests.
5. Users may be allowed only those minimal privileges necessary to complete the assigned job (the least privilege rule). "I am cleared, let me see that" is invalid.
6. Keep the design simple and the security programs as small as possible to allow effective testing and error elimination (this is called certification if carried out to its logical conclusion, i.e., proof that the system has no errors). The U.S. Department of Defense's "Trusted Systems Evaluation Criteria" (CSC 001–83) is useful in this connection.

7. Privileges should be separated: two people must authorize an action or prove a result.
8. Shared access processes should be minimized because they can allow unplanned information paths. Each individual user must have a unique identity and specific access and operational rights to establish personal accountability clearly.

The Process of Access Control

There is really no reason we should not use the awesome power of the computer to provide really effective security. Since the mid-1950s computer scientists and designers have talked about "human-friendly" systems. To date they have not delivered. Currently, state-of-the-art artificial intelligence systems deliver mind-boggling capabilities. But the perceived lack of interest on the part of customers and the cost of providing human-languagelike interfaces continues to deny the average computing user the comforts of dealing with a responsive AI system. (Appendix VIII describes a proposal for a human-friendly, consistently applied access control system.) There are few places where this is so true as in the use of security access controls. Usually this is a complex process; Figure 8.1 illustrates the flow of decisions, human and computer, in an effective access management system. These features are found in most systems, but not consistently or in friendly form.

For a number of years, government agencies and (to some degree) computer manufacturers have been working on improving the quality of system security controls. Generally, these efforts centered around such establishments as the Department of Defense Computer Security Center and the National Computing Center in the United Kingdom. They had to do with improving the effectiveness of the control software/hardware mechanisms to a point where a given system could be "certified" as being reliably secure. These efforts were concentrating on the *internals* of computing. That improvements have been made is evidenced by many good, reliable commercial security software products (RACF, ACF2, SECURE, TOP SECRET, and so forth). Promising work has also been done on provably secure systems, principally for military applications (Honeywell's MULTICS and SCOMP are examples).

Advanced access-control software systems often use special "certified" hardware. Such systems enforce strict rules to prevent unauthorized access:

A reference monitor checks all requests for service.

The system allows no reads up to higher security levels, and no writes down to lower security levels.

ACCESS MANAGEMENT

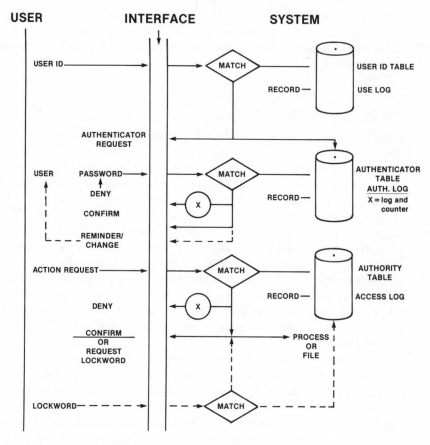

Figure 8.1 Logical access control process.

All rules are enforced through complete mediation.

The security system is in a "kernel," an isolated, protected, and certifiable (no software or engineering errors) section of the hardware/software.

The kernel has verifiable correctness.

In spite of great technical strides, the individual user continues to face a bewildering and confusing set of access procedures, especially if more than one make of terminal or personal computer is used.

Automated Logical Access Control System

In 1983 Charles R. Symons of Nolan Norton & Company, London (formerly of Rank Xerox), proposed an Automated Logical Access Control System or ALACS. ALACS addresses the human-machine interface, which is really the key to effective security. Symons asks "Why do we have to make security burdensome to people, especially those who use several different systems?" ALACS proposes using the power of the computer to motivate and assist the user in good security practices.

Recall Principle 3, which said that if the security system is unwieldy or costly users will find a way to go around it or nullify it. ALACS addresses that issue. For our purposes here, assume that the physical and procedural security elements typical of a given business situation are in place. For example, we do not anticipate that you will allow members of the public to casually saunter through your offices or sit down at your terminals and hack away. Given a reasonably controlled business environment, the logical security elements (hardware and software functions) can provide effective security control in a "friendly" manner, using currently available technologies. But the ALACS proposal goes further; it suggests that all computer manufacturers and software developers *standardize* these features. In his paper (see Appendix VIII), Symons points out that any of us (with a driver's license) can rent a car, and drive away without lessons. This is so because all automobiles have a standard layout—steering wheel, brake, clutch, accelerator, gear mechanism—so that we already know how to make the car go and how to control it, no matter the make or country of origin. The car's access and control system is standardized; you do not have to be a locksmith or mechanic to use it.

Unfortunately, the computer user does not have this luxury. Even within the same office and with systems equipment supplied by the same manufacturer, a clerical employee may be faced with different systems and system processes for customer administration, selling, inventory, deliveries, product servicing, and payroll. Each of these systems may use different terminal equipment and each may have unique security-control features, which means a different sign-on process for each. Any wonder that we see notes stuck up on the wall telling "How to sign on to this system" and conveniently including the supposedly secret password?

Why should these processes not be standardized? They need not be identical, but a similar process will both save work and simplify tasks, and will markedly improve security by (1) encouraging good security practices on the part of system users and (2) enforcing proper security discipline in terms of password construction, frequency of password changes, and the like.

Remember that Principle 2 said that the design of a security system must not be secret. There is no security in confusion.

The Process

Within the access control process we have three separate activities:

1. Identification: the claim to be a certain person or program.
2. Authentication: the proof of the identity claimed in Step 1 through something (the "token") the claimant has, is, or knows; in today's systems this token is usually a password, but plastic cards, voiceprints, hand-geometry measurements, and even retina scans will become more common in the near future.
3. Authorization: approval of the authenticated accessor to do specific things and only those things, per our least-privilege rule.

Operation

The computer can assist the user in a friendly way and at the same time require that user to practice good security discipline. The ALACS control process described in Appendix VIII is a simple, straightforward process. The computer itself encourages the user to practice good security. The standardization of the process, with eventual consistent and effective password across systems and applications, will make secure use of the computer convenient and simple.

An alternative to software security—or, better, a supplement to such systems, is the call-back or source-of-request verification control mechanism, usually an electronic control between the modem and the network. Figure 8.2 illustrates the workings of one of these products.

Decentralization of Access Management

An important benefit from the access control software packages now offered (such as SECURE, ACF-2, RAC-F, TOP SECRET), which can be adapted to many of the ALACS techniques, is the opportunity to decentralize the security-control function. That is, the software enables a large organization to place responsibility and capability for the granting, denial, and modification of access authorities at field units or local offices. As use of computers increases, especially at the personal workstation level, the security-management load at a central data center becomes intolerable and the bureaucratic delays in servicing access authority approval/denial requests become unacceptable to operating business activities. Consider a business with fifty branches and a thousand authorized computer users. If only 10 percent of the users have job changes, authority changes, or system access problems, the central security officer must validate (by getting proof of identity and management authorization for each action) and process 100

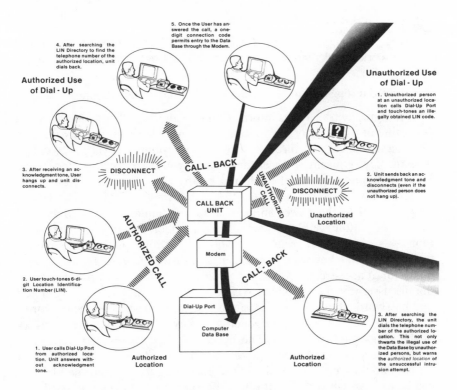

Figure 8.2 Dial-up access control system. (*Source*: LeeMAH Security systems, Hayward, Calif., reprinted with permission.)

requests. These changes are made via a special security officers' code on an authorized terminal. A special security terminal can be put in the branch office, with an appropriate subset of security authority, and the tasks becomes more manageable. The local controller, office manager, or similar executive can accommodate business-required changes much more efficiently, have authority proofs at hand, and avoid the errors always found in paper transfers. Further, having responsibility for access control at the local level places responsibility for ensuring the integrity of the branch's business data where it belongs.

Encryption

Probably the most promising security technology involves the science of cryptography, or information transformation. Encryption can provide highly effective protection for information, which might be

Stolen on disks or tapes

Accessed through software attacks (see Chapter 6) or communications/
network attacks via terminals, which gives entry to data files on on-
line disks

Accessed through wiretaps or radio interceptions of data communications.

Cryptography transforms information into an unintelligible form of data
consisting of a randomly substituted stream of bits. Cryptography is based
on a mathematical structure (algorithm) that produces an output based on
a secret key, typically a large number. A typical key is that used in the
Data Encryption Standard published by the U.S. Bureau of Standards;
this DES key has 56 bits and 8 parity bits, which allow users of the system
to generate 2 to the power 56 keys: a number equal to that represented
by the digit 2 followed by 56 zeros. That number illustrates why cryptography is such a robust security method; even with a powerful computer,
testing for such a key would require years of work. Cryptography can also
be useful in access control systems to ensure the secrecy of passwords. In
the discussion of the simplified ALACS access control systems we noted
that passwords should be stored in the system in one-way encrypted form.
In such a system the computer generates a key from certain characteristics
of the user sign-on situation. The password is stored in encrypted form.
When the correct password is entered, the computer matches the encrypted
forms. Should a penetrator obtain the encrypted forms from the file they
will be useless: when passed through the encryption process, they will not
match.

Where encryption is used, data security is a function of key security.
Keys never appear outside the cryptographic subsystem in most encryption
systems except for a brief time when keys are loaded. Keys are handled
within the system in encrypted form. We therefore have two types of keys:
Data keys are used to encrypt information, and key-encrypting keys are
used to encrypt other keys. These latter keys occur in two forms, session
keys and master keys. The master key identifies an authorized node on a
network; the session key, encrypted by the master key, secures one set of
information en route over a network. The management and control of keys
is therefore a most serious matter. Effective encryption systems provide
for key management in clever ways that involve human actions only
minimally.

When an application program stores information on a tape or disk file,
the encryption can be performed at the direction of application software.
The encryption requires computer cycles to process the encoding activity
but is transparent to the process. Special care must be taken to protect the
key: as data that cannot be decrypted are irretrievably lost. Usually, the
application program will "call" an encryption subroutine, which does the
encrypting work and provides for a recoverable key for later use in infor-

mation retrieval. The key may be derived from characteristics of the file, the process (for example, date/time), or a combination therefore. Alternatively, the key may be manually entered via a special key entry device; a risk exists in such cases that the manually set key may be lost.

Public Key Encryption

In 1977, three scientists at the Massachusetts Institute of Technology— Ronald Rivest, Adi Shamir, and Len Adelman—developed the concept for an encryption method that would allow users to publish keys much as telephone numbers are published in directories. Such a system would allow the user to send a message with proof ("signed message") of its authenticity; to send a confidential message with assurance that only the recipient could read it, even if many others got the message by any method; and to use encryption as a privacy tool without the need to establish complex key-management schemes. The Public Key Cryptosystem (Rivest, Shamir, and Adelman, 1977) uses the properties of very large prime numbers to provide each user with a "public" key and a "private" key. The system is based on the fact that, given a product of very large prime numbers, it is impossible with known mathematical techniques to determine the factors of such a number. The Public Key system is now being developed for practical use and in the future will provide a valuable security tool.

Encryption has been a disappointment to the manufacturers and developers of encryption software and hardware. Business managers have not seen fit to spend the considerable sums often required for encryption; however, costs will go down as encryption technology improves and unit sales increase, as security concerns develop in relation to the perceived and actual threats. Today's managers should be more concerned about information on pieces of paper. Tomorrow will be another story, as the information age unfolds. For example, the use of radio telecommunications (the satellite and dish antenna systems so often used today) requires encryption of all traffic for any reasonable level of security.

Personal Workstation Security

In my *Protecting Information in the Electronic Workplace* (1983) I discussed in detail the wide variety of computing hardware and applications for use at the personal workstation. The most common example of this phenomenon is the personal computer. Technology can provide superior information control and security when using the personal computer or any of the many workstation products. The problem is that most of us are too lazy or careless really to bother.

The situation is not unlike that involving safe-deposit boxes, as already pointed out. One tends to keep at home many things that should be locked away, but the act of going to the bank and getting into the safe-deposit box is troublesome at best. So we "take a chance" and keep valuables around the house.

The personal computer involves unusual risks, described at length in Chapter 2. But there are also effective security elements available, if personal computer users will only apply them. To sum up this point:

1. Because of its power and especially its communications capabilities, the personal computer and its information storage elements present severe vulnerabilities.
2. These vulnerabilities are made worse because the personal computer is frequently used outside the normal, controlled business environment— where rules cannot be enforced and where unknown persons often can have access.
3. Nevertheless, if carefully used with the controls and software available for the purpose, the personal computer can provide better security than that typically provided to information on paper.

The communication capability of the personal computer presents the most severe security risk. Unknown persons can potentially break into central files or local computer files, or observe or change information in the process of being communicated. It is probably unrealistic to expect that people are not going to use the easiest, most effective methods to gain information and to do their work. So we begin by making an assumption: *People will use microcomputers at home, and they will use telecommunications services to connect with central computers and network services.*

Given that assumption, we must try to limit the damage an unauthorized person can do. Viewing the personal computer as a terminal, the ALACS processes described in Appendix VIII apply, implemented at the central computer site. Each user must be identified, the claimed identity authenticated, and then only authorized actions allowed. Further, the personal computer user must be required to use all the security features available and must be motivated to follow good security discipline. This means

1. Using effective passwords (not easily guessed, of at least six characters in length, changed at least every ninety days).
2. Using appropriate file lockwords, or preferably encryption, when a fixed disk is in use; these lockwords should not be easily guessable.
3. Removing and locking away floppy disks when not in use.
4. Using encryption when appropriate for very high-value information, both during transmission and when data are stored on disks or tapes; encryption is the only effective protection against traffic copying or interference through wiretaps or radio interception. Several encryption software packages are already available for microcomputer users (Highland, 1984). Situations where telecommunications encryption is appro-

priate include strategic planning, funds transfer, product research, financial reporting, and market strategy applications, where the implications of information loss or interference with messages are severe. Requirements for privacy may also justify encryption.

5. Avoiding printouts where unnecessary and destroying unneeded printouts by shredding or burning; remember that in Chapter 2 we noted that theft of information on paper is the most frequent and obvious situation. Wastepaper is a fruitful source for industrial espionage agents. Properly mark and store all critical reports.

6. Protecting media (tapes and disks) and documents when enroute or in public places.

These good security practices must be used *at home* as well as at the office.

At the central computer site, which might be a minicomputer in an office as well as in a data center, risks can be controlled by limiting telephone dial-up as a means of access from personal computers. The security measures include:

1. Setting up a telecommunications "front end" microcomputer that can screen inward calls and authenticate users before they are connected to the database computer; upon receiving a call, the front-end computer requires a special password for further processing.

2. Using a front-end computer to establish a special permissions control. In this case, a personal computer user who wishes to access the central computer must request special permission. This permission, when granted, includes a password good for only a specified time, such as twenty four hours. This type of control limits the "window of vulnerability" even in cases where the personal computer operator is careless and allows teenage children or others to observe the password.

3. Requiring a preliminary call and a call-back to establish a connection. This ensures that the remote personal computer is in fact at the telephone number and location described by the authentic user employee. The call-back can be manual (made by a computer operator at the central site) or automated through use of any of several "black boxes" now on the market (see Figure 8.2).

4. For high-security requirements situations, the business can forbid dial-up communications and install private circuits. This is usually too expensive for other than high-volume circuits, so is usually inappropriate for personal computing applications. Wiretap interceptions remain a risk even in this case.

The microcomputer has moved the computer's power to the personal level and has made the access mechanism portable. Many systems users will be working at home and, eventually, from public places such as computing booths in airports. Business managers must motivate employees to practice good security discipline in the use of computers.

Local Area Networks

The local area network or LAN is a high-speed network covering a limited area (perhaps a campus) and connecting terminals, microcomputers, and specialized devices. Such a network is connected to the "outside world" via the commercial networks through a special interface. Personal computer users connected to a LAN have very powerful capabilities for creating, moving, and storing files, doing graphics, and communication via message systems with other LAN users, and also have available both personal and centralized files. The general rules proposed above also apply to LAN users. But there are some special requirements, which include the provision of public, shared, and private files on the file servers connected, so that users may define the persons authorized to view files or perform processes. And since LANs may have high-speed printers that are shared among many users, a means is required to suppress printing of sensitive documents until proper control can be assured; this may be done by requiring that the user come to the printer and enter a password to start printing. Finally, LAN cables laid outside areas of control—such as through the spaces occupied by another company—should be put in conduits to prevent a casual physical connection that could allow copying of all traffic. (For detailed information, see my *Protecting Information in the Electronic Workplace*.)

Practical Operating Details

By its nature, this book is a theory text that talks about concepts and management approaches and organizations. But there is a practical side to electronic security. At this point we will consider actions that should be taken to provide minimal safeguards for business information processed or communicated by computer systems. There are a number of essential elements in providing protection. Management may decide to go further, to provide additional safeguards for high-value data, but these are the basics:

1. Formally assign people with sufficient technical capabilities to identify, develop or buy, and install security software suitable to your system and applications. Asking someone to do this job on an ad hoc basis immediately compromises the effort; such an assignment tells everyone that management is not serious about security. Assigning a capable full-time employee does wonders for motivation, which is what the security game is all about. Make sure the employee selected has the experience and capacity to do the job. For medium to large companies we are probably talking about a job-midpoint salary of $35,000 at minimum for the electronic security consultant. (See the organization chart in Figure 9.2.)

2. Provide sufficient budget to allow the function to do its job. An initial investment in software is usually necessary. This will be $50,000 to $100,000 per site for software packages or for development of your own access control system (*not* recommended).

3. Carefully review the computer system uses and the classification of the information processed (there is not much point in starting until information valuation has been accomplished) by both individual users and data center-operated programs. Identify all the possible access means and the controls presently in place. With the help of your computer supplier, identify the security elements available from the currently used software and hardware.

4. Establish a benchmark security position and work to meet that level of control. Your benchmark will be based on the classification levels you have assigned to your information and the risks you wish to accept (see Chapters 3 and 4). These are prerequisites to any successful program.

5. You may need to purchase or develop incremental security software for unique circumstances such as for encryption. If you have a popular brand of computer, the software may be any one of several proven packages, including those offered by the manufacturer. The Computer Security Institute of Northborough, Mass., offers regular courses on selection of security software. Professional groups can also help.

6. Careful installation of the package is essential. Your implementation of the software can make the difference between effective security and a sham. The default (that is, when no decision about access authorization has been made) must always be to a secure situation. If no decision has been made, the system denies access to everyone and every program. An effective system will work in a fashion similar to that described in Appendix VIII.

7. Authorizations for access must come from the data owner, usually a functional manager, and never from the data center management. (Consider a bank: the manager with the vault combination does not sign the disbursement vouchers.) Further, responsibility for maintaining security software must be carefully and specifically delineated from responsibilities for maintenance of operating system software. The two functions provide an check on the actions, one of the other.

8. Establish sufficient administrative positions, or consider decentralization so that an efficient response can be made to requests for security services such as initialization or cancellation of access authorities. If system users perceive security to be a burden and a barrier to operation, they will find ways to thwart your controls.

Communications

Dial-up access is always convenient to users and hence is very popular. It is also a great risk, as a dial-up system is literally available to anyone with a telephone. The alternatives are as follows, all *incremental* to the access control software described above:

1. Take the risk. This is not advised. Intelligent microcomputer users can test hundreds of telephone numbers and they will find yours shortly.

2. Use only direct leased line connections. This is very expensive unless you have only a few such connections, and even then security is not ensured, as wiretaps are fairly simple once the correct line is identified.
3. Install a communications front-end computer with security software. This computer can screen incoming calls and limit access to persons with special time-date authorizations (for example, the system will allow user A access only from 8:00 A.M. Tuesday to 12 noon Wednesday). This type of control can be set to meet variable user requirements. This does not remove all the risk but it severely cuts down the window of vulnerability.
4. Install call-back systems on each line, as described in Figure 8.2. This is probably the best alternative in terms of effective protection, but the cost may be significant.

High-Value Information

Encryption is the ultimate protection, and the only really reliable method for ensuring the security of critical, high-value data.

Consider point-to-point encryption of traffic on high-density telecommunications circuits that frequently carry high-value traffic. This requires a modest one-time investment (about $40,000 per circuit, multiplexed), and provides trouble-free protection from wiretaps or radio interceptions.

Provide an encrypting software utility program that applications programs can call to encrypt high-value data being written to disk or tape. Several such packages are available in the software market; do not try to write your own, as this is highly specialized work and homemade encryption systems have a 100-percent failure rate, in my experience.

Finally, continue to support the security effort with *management interest*.

9 | Information Security Management Functions

Protecting business information is only a part of a much larger responsibility for organizing and managing the business information resource. But since information security is a primary concern of this book, we will devote a chapter to considering the organizational place and functioning of the information security activity. Identifying, structuring, and valuing the information resource is the responsibility of the information resource executive (the Vice President/Information Resource Management or equivalent). Protection of business resources is properly assigned to the director or manager of security, who must respond to the information resource values assigned by the information resource manager. In doing so, the security director must develop or cause to be developed and apply such security measures as are appropriate to a resource of equivalent value. Figure 9.1 shows the top levels of an IRM organization, with special attention to the detail of the supporting security activity.

An important observation here: Very often the business information security effort is hopelessly squandered because the organizational responsibilities are poorly defined or never made clear. Examples include:

1. Where the systems manager has a computer security function but there is no information valuation program.
2. Where the director of security had responsibility for protecting the business but the information systems department has its own "special" security program.
3. Where computer output reports are marked and protected but the same information in typewritten form is handled in casual manner.

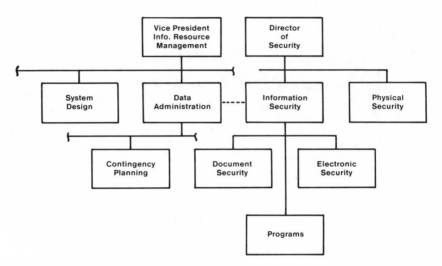

Figure 9.1 Organization for information security.

All these cases (and the others you may be thinking about) result from management ignorance about the importance of information. The purpose of this book, as noted often earlier, is to start management thinking about the information age.

To make the program work, the essential information resource management steps outlined in earlier chapters are prerequisites. Although the exact organizational placements of the functions described are relatively unimportant, it is *critical* that all responsibilities be assigned and organized in a way that provide for smoothly functioning information valuation, control, and protection. Management must face a number of organizational issues when deciding to protect business information, and even more important issues when the information security function is to work properly within the IRM function.

Security as such has traditionally had to do with the protection of the physical plant and assets of a business, and security is often thought of in terms of facilities or premises services. When we begin to consider information as an important asset, we have significantly broadened the scope of the security responsibility. And, the introduction of computers as *the* way to handle information has added a new requirement, that of technical capability. The traditional business-security function, with guards, gates, identity badges, and the like, was not equipped to deal with the sophistication of the information systems world. The ready solution adopted by most managements was to establish a computer-security responsibility within the information systems function.

But, as we have seen, this is the wrong view; computers are not the valuable, critical resource. Rather, information, in its mental, written, and electronic forms is the critical asset. In many companies we see an ineffective program resulting from the divergent activities of (1) computer security, with emphasis on protecting the data center; (2) information security, with emphasis on the typewritten page; and (3) physical security, looking after general plant and personnel security.

The emergence of IRM as a major management task changes the way management considers these functions. These changes include:

1. Information security appears as an important and major security activity, covering information in all its forms: written, electronic, and mental.
2. Physical security continues to be responsible for plant and personnel security.

Information Security Organization

In line with management recognition of information as a vital business resource, information security responsibility is placed as a separate, important function under the senior security manager. The information security function has staff relationships with the data management, information systems, and records management activities within IRM (described in Chapters 4 and 5). Also, information security has close working ties with the physical security function in the large-business security department. In smaller businesses, the organization should be set up to make best use of the talent available; however, clear-cut definition of responsibilities is essential.

The manager, information security, should be an experienced computer systems technologist. This employee should have experience in data processing operations and an understanding of operating systems functions. An auditing background would also be helpful. Educational requirements should include one of the following: mathematics, computer science, accounting, or industrial engineering, and an MBA would be beneficial. This is a significant job. In the United States, salary ranges for such a job would be $35,000 to $85,000, depending on company size.

Within the information security organizational subunit of the corporate security department, we can suggest several distinct responsibilities. These are subjective selections; management may wish to vary the task assignments according to individual employee capabilities or to fit company operational arrangements. Figure 9.2 shows the information security function in detail.

The term *consultant* (as in electronic security consultant) was chosen for use in this prototypical organization because the positions should be filled by professionals, people with significant experience and with design and implementation capabilities. The term as used indicates a senior-level em-

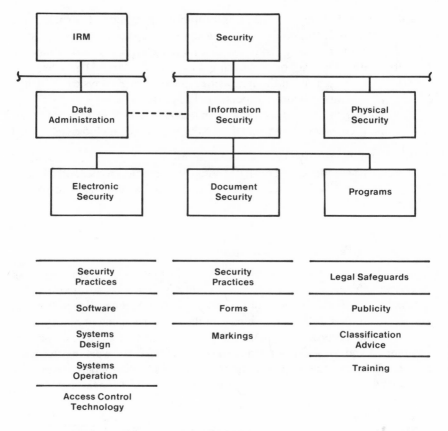

Figure 9.2 The information security function.

ployee. Reader should use those titles appropriate to the business practices in their particular industry, location, or situation.

Before we discuss the functional requirements of the parts of the information security function, we should recall that a precondition to information management is the assignment of value, or classification, of information. Management must have established and operated a process to identify high-value information and to categorize and mark such information so that it can be handled and protected properly. Any effort to organize an information-protection effort without information classification is doomed to failure: we cannot protect everything. Classification is the first essential step in the mandatory assignment of scarce resources for protection of information.

These decisions, and the initial start-up of the information classification process, are the responsibility of the IRM executive. In practice, however, this effort is usually carried out by the functional data owner assisted by the information security manager. The task includes:

1. Development and publication of information security policy, including information classification rules.
2. Project development and management to ensure that the initial classification effort is successfully completed.
3. Further organizational work to provide for program maintenance.

Referring to Figure 9.2, we shall discuss the various functions within the information security responsibility. In practice these may be combined, but we consider them separately for clarity.

Document Security

The document security function develops and publishes the rules and procedures for handling valued information in written or printed form. (Currently, this form represents the highest risk; see Chapter 2.) These activities include:

1. Developing classification nomenclature, valuation rules, and operating guidelines. These rules would explain (a) who is authorized to classify information, (b) definitions of classified information, and (c) situations when classification decisions are appropriate. This is important initial input to the standards.
2. Developing standards for marking and handling, including stamp designs (logos), document-control numbering practices, rules for destruction or downgrading, and the like. This responsibility includes rules for documents produced on computers.
3. Establishing special procedures for control of technical, research, engineering, and other documents with particular protection needs.

In addition, the document security consultant serves as an ongoing resource for the questions and problems that come up across the business in the daily operations. The consultant also participates in security investigations, usually conducted by the physical security manager, concerning information theft, leakage, purloined documents, and so on.

If the business includes government contracts, this function may also have responsibility for the appropriate government-directed industrial security program. In the United States, this program is established by the Department of Defense Industrial Security Manual DOD 5220.22M, which is an excellent reference for information security and control concepts.

Electronic Security

This function includes all information in electronic form processed or stored on computers and communications systems, including office automation systems. There is obviously a wide overlap among the functions within the information security area; careful coordination is required to make certain that operating practices are consistent for both computer-generated information and manually prepared documents. The electronic information security activity is directed toward technology—which, as we have seen, is the essential driving force for IRM. Among other responsibilities, the electronic security consultant

1. Develops and publishes security rules and procedures for all users of electronic information systems, personal workstations, networks, communications systems, and similar.
2. Designs and publishes marking and handling rules, such as video display markings and automatic generation of computer printer output markings (consistent with those established for noncomputer-printed documents), handling of computer-generated outputs in special cases such as bulk shipments of classified reports, and logical file headers to flag classification and cause proper control during processing, storage, or communications.
3. Establishes management control and rules for operation and interconnection of business computers, connections with outside computers or devices, home computing or communication of business information, and other special or innovative applications (see the discussion of personal computing in Chapter 2).
4. Develops procedures for maintaining security in data centers, laboratories, engineering centers, and other sites where computers are a major part of the normal operation. In conjunction with the physical security manager, writes facility security regulations for special computer-use sites such as data centers.
5. Develops and publishes standards for the guidance of systems analysts and programmers; works closely with the systems development activity to assist in resolving information security issues of design and processing controls.
6. Works with the physical security manager as required to investigate suspected computer/communication misuse or crime.

Program Consultants and Mental Information

We have mentioned the requirement for employee understanding and motivation several times. When a manager takes a microcomputer home and does work connected via a network to central computers, the security of the business information (including all that stored on central database files) relies almost totally on the manager's integrity and loyalty. The program function is responsible for continuing motivation and training activities across all the information forms. This function must especially address exposures from carelessness with mental and orally expressed information. While this might look like attempts at thought control, it is not that at all. But it does reflect a need for increased awareness and motivation among employees, who always have information in their heads and who may be tempted to boast a little—and perhaps carelessly.

Among these responsibilities are:

1. Development and presentation of training programs, including films, slide shows, training aids, and the like.
2. Development and use of motivational aids (posters, calendars, rulers, folders, paperclip holders, other office miscellaneous items with security markings).
3. Warehousing and control of the publications, materials, and the like needed for continuing operation of the program.
4. With assistance from the general counsel and personnel department, ensure that appropriate legally binding agreements are executed to protect highly valued business information.

Field Organization in Large Business

The organization described above for the information security function may be replicated in a condensed version in operating units. We talked about security coordinators as a means of cascading the security message and functionality throughout the organization (Chapter 6). An option for conducting the information management function is through special assignments of security coordinators in the various operating groups. The specific tasks assigned in each case would relate to the jobs and processes in that organization. For example, in a systems group the primary task for the security coordinator would be electronic security, although other tasks could be assigned. In a large engineering organization, an engineer in each section is assigned one-year rotating responsibility as a security coordinator. After a while a cadre of people with considerable understanding and interest will have developed. This is a real benefit to the business in a sensitive product-development area.

Reading through the appendices will provide a detailed overview of the activities required of the information security subunit of the information resource management business function. The technology applications for security, largely the responsibility of the electronic security function, were described in Chapter 8.

10 | Information Resource Reliability Planning

> *The recovery process must be a by-product of the daily data-processing operation. As with a living creature, the system must be designed so that it recovers naturally from injuries. A small injury should be repairable easily and with little or no effect on performance. A catastrophic injury, such as an entire file being destroyed, will need more drastic measures, and the system will have to stop part of its work temporarily while the damage is rectified.*
>
> —James Martin (1969, p. 249)

Any critical business resource requires that management consider the effects of its unavailablility. For raw materials, a loss of supply could result from war or weather. Parts and components could be denied to the business because of strikes, transportation problems, or fire. Astute managers will have thought out such risks and provided planning, just in case. Some businesses spread orders for critical components among several suppliers to make sure that a single event will not destroy the resource supply.

Information is a critical business resource, and managers must be concerned with the continuing reliability and availability of business information. This usually involves the planning for alternative information systems infrastructure in event of a serious loss of facilities or capabilities and for the secure storage of replicated records.

Contingency planning is a general management responsibility that relates directly to the viability of the business. It occurs in many areas of business, including manufacturing, distribution, and raw materials supply. Information reliability planning is not a security matter any more than is the planning of alternative raw materials sources. The practice of assigning planning for computing systems contingencies to a security manager reflects the concept, prevalent in the early days of computing, that all data belonged to the data center manager. If one accepts the essential function we have called information resource management, it is evident that information contingency planning is properly a role for the executive responsible for that resource.

There are two major aspects to information contingency planning. The first concerns the replacement of processing, storage, and communications resources; the second has to do with replication of critical information elements for safekeeping. The latter responsibility is closely associated with the records management function, one of the activities in an information resource management program.

Effective management thinking about information contingency is often clouded by the worries engendered by the great computer-crime scare mentioned in Chapter 1. One is hard-pressed to find a happy medium among managers responsible for information contingency planning. Perhaps that is so because computing history appears to have so many disasters. Software failures, hardware failures, design faults, implementation problems; the midnight telephone ring is a condition of employment for those of us in the data-processing "business." Yet a senior manager of a large government operation once solemnly informed an auditor that his organization had no contingency plan because "we really haven't had any disasters." Opposite from this Hobson's-choice example we have the corporation that decided to spend hundreds of thousands of dollars preparing for a contingent event with an estimated probability of once in five hundred years.

As business managers we must achieve a balanced position between these extremes of pessimism and optimism. Our contingency plans must recognize that we simply cannot avoid some ill effects from a disaster, should one come upon us. Our task with the information resource management structure is to identify what we can do, at minimum cost and given our management's proclivity to risk-taking, to control the aftermath. As with security matters, we have to recognize that it is seldom possible to avoid ill effects completely, should a disaster occur. We must strive to minimize the *business effects*, at the lowest possible cost. Too often, the wrong people are planning for information contingencies; their interest is in the computer hardware, and they lack the broad view necessary to recognize the business effect of the possible event and its results. That is why contingency planning must be done by senior managers, not by junior staff involved with security aspects. The IRM executive should assign a senior manager to this task.

Note that in the early stages of planning the question is not "What should we do to ensure continuing operations?" We are not yet at that point of decision. Keep in mind the principles we discussed in considering risk management in Chapter 7. Contingency planning should reflect the risk-taking position of our executive management. Also, the contingency plan should be a part of the total information resource management approach, including the use of insurance and self-insurance on a planned basis.

Management must answer the question "How much risk are we willing to take?" The reply is basic to all contingency planning, since an immediate total replacement of any major resource is impractical. Both cost and replacement availability make a short-term total-recovery plan, in case of a major disaster, unrealistic. Some businesses, such as airlines and insurance companies, can justify maintenance of a full duplicate facility: the businesses of these companies would be destroyed without a continuing information-handling capability.

Management willingness to take risk must be a guide to the use of insurance as a hedge against the final contingency plan—and to the approach used to plan for emergency reactions. A general set of guidelines can be offered to managers responsible for information resource contingency planning:

1. Top management must specify the risk-acceptance posture of the business. The company's risk manager (the insurance executive) should be key to this decision. Purchased insurance and self-insurance can offset much expense in contingency preparation. Certain service industries in which the business is widely dispersed may be totally self-insuring and thus have no contingency planning needs.
2. The information resource manager, the key executive responsible for information-using functions, must make beforehand decisions on information recovery priorities. Most businesses that do not have effective plans in place have failed to do so because efforts have foundered on the inability to resolve this point. These are top-level decisions; middle managers are typically unwilling to make realistic decisions about prioritizing information needs because to accept a lower priority would admit to a lesser degree of importance. The functional executives making or providing input to these decisions should be provided with cost guidelines so that alternatives can be selected on a business basis. For example, what is the exposure from paying employees based on past history rather than on actual hours? Would the cost of a premium overpayment be more or less than the cost of providing positive recovery capability for payroll processing? Senior management should understand clearly that this process is one of reducing and controlling risk, not one of avoiding risk. The difficult process of selecting the few most critical business information flows for contingency preparation is so important that all planning work should stop here until selection is completed. An "almost-everything" answer is not an answer at all. No business can afford such a posture; it would be like insuring for every contingency with no deductibles.
3. The minimum critical resource (MCR) must be identified, based on the priorities developed in Step 2. This is the minimum information resource with attendant processing infrastructure (not necessarily the same as computing) required to support the essential minimum information needs for the business. These will be the top few functional information flows identified by the information resource manager and approved by top management. The company's information-element inventory, noted as the first essential to information resource management in Chapter 3, is

the reference for consideration in such a decision. The value judgments expressed in terms of information classification are also important indicators. The contingency plan must be such as to provide, in some reasonable alternate form, the minimum critical resource. The MCR must be available on notice; that is not the same as instantaneously, but in some cases—such as for an on-line reservations system—recovery capability must be very quick. The MCR is difficult to figure out for most large businesses, as many information flows interconnect. Various capabilities (including telecommunications, disk capacity, and process loads) must be considered. MCR represents the recoverability "kernel" essential to a workable plan. Fortunately, most large computer suppliers can respond rather effectively to emergency needs. Manual processing may be an acceptable stop-gap measure. In the short term, one of the recovery centers now established may offer continuity. Some businesses have set up replicated processing centers. But keep in mind that computing equipment is only part of the needed resource, and may not even be the critical part. Employees who are key to operations may be unavailable after an emergency; capable substitute people may be essential to the success of your plan. Too, normal data collection systems may not be working after a disaster; alternative ways to generate raw information may also be critical plan elements.

4. A detailed plan, with all necessary arrangements made and contracted for in advance, is next. The plan must leave nothing to doubt. It should read like the script of a play; the principal parts must be assigned to reliable employees who understand their roles. Various information resource management activities such as records retention (for back-up files) are important in this process. The plan must specify all the functions; contractual obligations; and sequential, timed movement of people, data, and materials necessary. Specific responsibilities must be assigned by name (the use of teams is good because some employees may be on holiday or ill or may have been injured in the emergency).

5. The plan must be tested under the most realistic conditions possible. An unbiased referee or monitor from outside the responsible organization (perhaps an auditor) must observe all aspects of the test, make detailed notes of problems, and report on the general efficiency. Contingency plans must then be reviewed and changes made to correct problems. A realistic test means that the crew doing the test is completely separated from any resource that is normally present. It is common to assume that clerical help, various miscellaneous unidentified files, and the like will be available. Not necessarily so in an emergency. The test should force out unusual circumstances; in a real emergency, Murphy's Law that "everything which can go wrong will" will always apply.

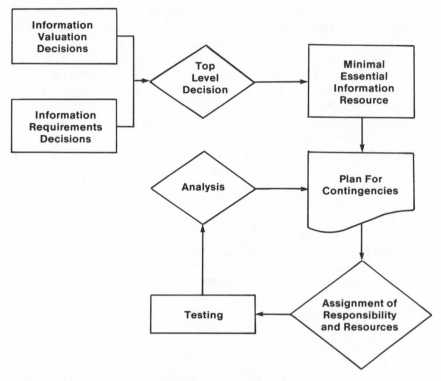

Figure 10.1 Flow and components of the new contingency plan.

A rule of thumb is that a well-tested, superbly documented contingency plan has a 70-percent chance of total success. Anything less is mere wishful thinking. Prospects rapidly deteriorate. Figure 10.1 illustrates the contingency planning process.

Cases

Over a period of time as a military inspector general and as a civilian consultant to industry, I have observed many contingency recovery exercises. Some were particularly memorable, and in retrospect amusing.

A European business kept its recovery computer tapes in an ancient vault. During a test, the equally ancient caretaker of the plant site containing the vault was unable to open the even more ancient lock. (The key weighed about three pounds.) A locksmith had to be summoned—not part of the plan.

A multinational corporation planned to recover and continue processing in a data center in a distant country, commuting there by air. Once airborne, it was discovered that the particular processing instructions needed had not been brought along. And no parachutes were at hand.

A company in New York City selected and contracted with a nearby data center for use of a computer for contingency purposes. The computer was the same model and used the same operating system; however, during the initial test, most programs simply would not run properly. The vendor was unable to fix or explain the problems. Another site had to be selected.

During contingency recovery tests, employees had to travel about ten miles to a warehouse to pick up safety tapes and disks. Because these media had not been properly identified and organized at the warehouse, several trips failed to produce everything needed and the test failed.

A large corporation arranged for a contingency test at a back-up site about fifty mile distance from the home processing center. Upon arrival at the site by automobile, the computer operations staff realized that they had left behind several elements essential to operations—including various "fix-it" decks of alternate JCL (control cards). The systems didn't run well even at home; a first consideration for data processing staff is that the systems to be moved in an emergency be well documented and operate smoothly.

On reflection, we see that the information resource contingency preparation is very much like systems development. We ask what does the customer (in this case, top management) want? We recognize a limit to what we can provide. If we do good systems analysis, we suggest alternatives if more reasonable, practical, or economic means are to be found. Then we construct a framework and document it in detail. Finally, the process is exhaustively tested, with careful records kept to ensure correction of the most minute problem.

The IRM executive must recognize that business is a risk-taking enterprise, that we cannot avoid risk. We want to limit unacceptable risks and preserve the really essential information flows necessary to continued business viability. The business risk manager knows that certain classes of risks should be borne as a matter of doing business, because insurance costs are too high. Similarly, within the business information resource pool there are data elements that could be done without. We should not be advising management to expend resources on contingency planning for nonessential information. Rather, the information contingency plan should provide for maintaining essential business processes, at the lowest possible cost.

11 | What to Do, *Now*

> *As we move into the information age of the 1980s, the new breed of information managers will become integrated into the business they serve by working more closely with users and senior management in solving their needs, will marshall their information resources for the solution of business problems and in support of management, and will move up the corporate ladder as their firms' chief information officers.*
>
> —*William R. Synott and William H. Gruber (1981, p. 12)*

We have suggested some management and organizational concepts that will require significant effort and you may be saying "I'm not ready for all that yet." But history moves along with or without us, and the information age is here.

So in this chapter we will provide a few practical recipes for beginning information protection through IRM. From these, management can obtain some relative degree of comfort about information resource security. (The appendixes offer examples of policies, procedures, and checklists to help begin the process of managing your business information resource.)

Critical First Steps

To get started, consider these management actions:

1. Take a macro view of your business; think about the big picture. What are your long-range strategic goals? How does information, any kind of business information, contribute to those goals?
2. Identify the critical information elements that may be essential to meeting your business goals. Value these critical elements on some relative scale. (You may well have only two classifications. No matter, you are deciding what is necessary to protect.)
3. Establish an information resource management responsibility at the executive level. Organize to bring your essential information elements under control.
4. Make practical decisions on protecting these critical (now classified) information elements based on your estimate of their relative values.

5. Tell your employees what you expect of them in protecting business information. Failure to explicity establish your recognized information values, as well as the responsibilities of your employees, may leave you without legal standing should fraud or information damage occur.
6. Support the introduction of computer-related crime legislation in your state, if it has not already been provided. Laws do not prevent your being damaged by information crime, but they establish in people's minds that such things are illegal. Appendix VII is a proposed Act on Computer-Related Offenses prepared by an ad hoc committee for the Connecticut legislature in 1983.
7. Don't allow concern about computer-related crime to cause you to attempt quick fixes. Computer crimes are well publicized, but much more serious damage is done every day through inept system design, poor training, and malicious mischief. This is not to say that people do not commit crimes using computers or that the use of computers in business does not tempt miscreants. But there are many other, more common vulnerabilities we should address. In doing so we will also put up some barriers to make computer-related crime more difficult.

The need to recognize and manage the information resource is not limited to big business. Conceptually, the requirement exists in businesses of all sizes. As society moves ever more swiftly into the information age, all managers ignore information resources at their peril. Of course, the size of a business has strong bearing on the way in which an information resource management program is implemented. Most of the discussion within the text is appropriate for large corporations, but we should discuss appropriate actions for other sizes of business too.

Protecting Information Resources in a Small Business

By a small business we mean one with an annual gross revenue of $100,000 to $10 million. That smaller businesses are often the last to adopt computers doesn't mean that the business information resource is unimportant for them. Since the small business usually has a narrow product or service base, any attack on that base can be critical. Proprietary information that may provide a competitive advantage needs to be carefully protected. Business records must be well controlled and shielded, as far as practicable, from intentional or careless errors, malicious damage or loss, or unauthorized transfer to others.

Small business managers recognize the value of their business information. The requirement to establish information values is as important here as it is for a large company. This is true because it is impossible to provide good protection for everything. Many years ago, when Coca-Cola sales were just beginning, the founder took great care to maintain the secrecy of the product formula. Everyone knows of the success of that company, and to this day the formula is still a secret. We don't know what turns history might have taken if the formula had been stolen away, but we can assume that success would have been affected.

Although many businesspeople will say "we really don't have any secrets," a simple test will demonstrate the fallacy of the statement. Merely walk into any business office and start going through the files. There is always a concern for privacy and information integrity; at a minimum, this concern is supported by requirements of law.

Only fools make all their business matters public. So, even in the smallest of businesses there are information resources which need protecting. Generally, this protection consists of physical and procedural security elements. If a minicomputer or microcomputer is used, or if a computer service is purchased, logical security elements may be appropriate. We will suggest a set of vulnerabilities for the smaller business in order of lessening risk, then outline some protective measures.

Vulnerabilities of the Small Business

1. Malfeasance by a trusted employee, such as fraud, theft, or the like, based on privileged written information, business recordkeeping, other sensitive activities.
2. Misuse of such business records as customer files, market strategy, financial plans, for personal gain.
3. Unauthorized transfer of proprietary information concerning new products, product testing, market studies for new products.
4. Malicious theft, damage, or change of business records or important information.

Small Business Management of Information Resources

Small business can do a number of reasonable and simple things to safeguard its information. Among several worthwhile efforts are:

1. Establish your rights and interests in your business information by having all employees sign nondisclosure agreements; your legal counsel can assist in determining the correct form. Should an employee leave and take with him or her critical competitve information, these agreements may allow you to obtain a court order to prevent the former employee from using the information in competition with you.
2. Establish adequate controls over critical information and data. Follow good accounting practices. Any activity responsible for controlling cash, receivables, payables, negotiable instruments (or similar items) should have proof and review processes so that fraud or theft would require collusion by two or more employees.

3. If a computer is used either in-house or via a service bureau, make certain that audit trails and proofs usual to a manual system are installed. Do not accept that programs provided by others have integrity. Trace back all automated transactions to input documents; batch controls are a way to do this.

4. Avoid having in any one employee or consultant the only person who understands how a process works. Do not trust computer programmers to build a system to your specifications. Some second trusted party should always process a test case in detail; keep in mind that all computer software has bugs, some of which could be intentional. Insist on complete documentation for your system so that another person could make changes to the programs if necessary.

5. Identify your most valuable information. Keep it locked away when not in use. Mark it as being specially valuable; this may be important if you have to go to court. Train employees how to handle this special information. (In small businesses the process of classifying information may not be practical. Here we assume that the process is informal, with information elements being marked with or assigned descriptive notations by the business owner or corporate officers.)

6. If computers are used, teach employees to handle magnetic media (tapes, disks, and the like) with the same care they give written information. Tapes and disks should have value indications on the outside, the same as documents; this can be critical in a court test. You will probably have to prove that the information you are trying to recover or control was recognized by you as being valuable, and that you in fact marked and treated it differently from your casual business information. Media containing valuable information should be kept locked up when not in use. If data are retained on fixed magnetic disks that cannot be removed from the computer or drive unit for safekeeping, you have four alternatives for protecting valuable information on the disk:

   a. Copy all valuable data to a tape or removable floppy disk for storage and erase those files from the fixed disk.

   b. Use a software package to encrypt the valuable files on the fixed disk; you'll have to decrypt the data to use it, and remember that should you lose the code key you lose the data.

   c. Lock up the entire system in a cabinet when not in use. You could disconnect the disk drive and lock away that one unit, but that seems excessively difficult. There are special cabinets available that provide slide-in-and-out features for microcomputer users who wish to secure the system.

   d. Purchase a software package that allows you to password, or logically secure, files. This method has dangers in that any knowledgeable person who could start up the computer could manipulate the operating system to go around the password barrier.

7. If you use the services of a bureau or network, check with the supplier to make sure that you understand the security features available. *Use them.* Most suppliers of computing services have excellent security features (usually special software that the user may "call") built into the services offered. But use of the features is optional, and your employees will choose not to use them if you give the option. (All security requires a certain amount of work, and people want to make things as simple as possible.) Make sure that passwords are kept secret; a password taped to a terminal is merely another telephone number, available to anyone.

8. If you have extremely sensitive, high-value information such as securities trading orders, oilfield data, new-product technology, or the like, you should seriously consider using encryption—the most secure and rigorous protection available. For the smaller business with one computer, a software package can be obtained to encrypt data written to disk or tape files. If telecommunications security is a concern, encryption by use of hardware ("black boxes") is more cost-efficient: hardware encryption does not use up your costly computer cycles in the encypherment process. (Management of encryption keys, or codes, is essential and must be rigorous. Most modern systems provide for automated key management, so this should not be a big issue.)

In sum, the small business does have valuable information resources. These should be identified, managed, and protected in practical ways.

Protecting Information in a Medium-size Business

By medium-size businesses we mean those with gross revenues of $10 million to $100 million. The general approach and implementation activities described in Chapters 6 and 7 apply, except that the information resource management responsibilities may rationally be within the information systems organization. This must be done carefully so the proper objective view of information as a resource is maintained. Once top management has made the decision to go ahead with a program to protect information, the initial information management activity and valuation decisions will probably be made by senior functional managers. The concept of appointing part-time security coordinators as the implementing and maintaining means is attractive in medium-size businesses, where special assignments cannot be justified or afforded.

Medium-size businesses often get involved in "computer security"— defined as protection for the company data center. This is, as we've seen, only part of the problem. The effective information security program will address all aspects and forms of valuable information. Further, as computing power is distributed through personal computers and office automation, the data center becomes relatively less important. The overall information management and control efforts suggested in earlier chapters, with adjustments for the given business situation, is appropriate for middle-sized companies. Keep the end goal in mind: to conserve the information resource and ensure information integrity and reliability.

By emphasizing this goal, you'll be able to modify the full-scale program described in earlier chapters to meet your business needs. Some suggestions are:

1. Make the program a formal one, supported by appropriate top-management announcements. If the information resource is really important, it's worth doing the protection program in style. Half-hearted support is just kidding yourself; it's like locking the front door with a padlock when you have only a screen door in the rear.

2. Get the resources necessary to identify the important information, value it, and assign classification names. Publicize these names and the protective measures required. Employees should know that a document, computer printout, or presentation with certain markings requires them to use discretion and to take specific protective measures. Make sure that top value classifications do not exceed more than 1 percent or so of the total value information. The top value classification should be rigorously protected by issuing the information only to name-identified employees, storing in a vault, and by encryption for the storage or transmission of electronic forms. Only specifically authorized individual employees should be allowed access to the top value category.

3. Establish the business' rights to its proprietary information by using employee nondisclosure agreements, contractual agreements, or similar measures. Marking and special handing for information with competitive value is important; it may make the difference should legal remedies be necessary.

4. Give special attention to any circumstances in which company information could be misused. This includes accounting, order processing, any use of computers for financial purposes, and any distributed or personal computing. Set up effective controls and audit regularly. Remember that the risk of fraud or information theft using information on pieces of paper is much greater than the risk from electronic attack through a network or computer. The computer itself is a prolific paper generator. Make sure you know where computer printouts of valuable information are going. What happens to these documents after your employees are finished using them? What happens to scrap paper?

5. Apply reasonable electronic security measures in line with the established value of the information being processed. Be certain that classification indicators move along with the information as it travels through various manual and automated systems.

Figure 11.1 IRM organization and functions.

6. Tie in the audit and security responsibilities in the company with the information security programs, which must not be solely a systems and data processing exercise.

The appendixes provide examples of policies and standards that could be adapted for use in medium-size businesses.

Big Business

Any company in the *Fortune* 500 or equivalent group should consider the full information resource management effort as described in this book. Big businesses have big, complex information resource management needs. Specific responsibilities for control of the information resource must be assigned at a top executive level. Information protection should be a full-time job for at least one specialist, with other assignments as appropriate. At the same time, key functional managers whose responsibilities include the generation of valuable business information should have data-owner assignments related to information resource management. These responsibilities should encompass information valuation, monitoring information use, granting information and systems access authorizations, systems design review, and establishing and reviewing security and control measures. In large businesses the challenge is enormous, but there exist significant resources on which to draw.

Figure 11.1 shows an IRM organization and functions for a large business. These functions are present in an IRM activity in all businesses, but may not be assigned to separate functions in all cases. The appendixes offer many illustrations of the policies, procedures, and practices surrounding information management. They will help you understand the necessary actions to begin effective management control of your information resource.

I | Cases

Many instances of fraud, information theft, and the use of computers for unauthorized purposes have been reported in the daily press and in professional journals. Less attention has been given to cases involving inept or uncoordinated systems design, resulting in information "glut," loss of control, or duplication of effort. These illustrate the current situation and the need for information resource management better than theory.

The circumstances and names in these cases are changed, but they actually occurred during twenty-nine years in data processing, auditing, and security work. Many were reported by professional acquaintances, and some involved government agencies.

MIS

Company S manufactured and sold computing systems. During the period that management information system (MIS) was the vogue, S developed a network of terminals for its top executives. Each manager had a little system guide that explained how to retrieve and process certain information elements from the company's central files. These could be assembled into standard reports. The executive could also develop "custom" programs that would supposedly generate answers to specific management concerns by processing information drawn from the central data files. Surprisingly, the system actually worked. But the results were not as planned. Since the executives of S were very intelligent people, each conceived of various customized reports that would answer their unique management needs. But since the information input to these custom-built processes, and the processes themselves, were all different, the conclusions of the executives also differed. At top-level meetings numerous reports passed around "proved" varying viewpoints. Confusion and disagreement resulted. No consensus could be had.

Analysis

S management had failed to control the use of an important resource—information. This failure involved a lack of definition of the meaning, purpose, and intended use of information elements. Further, system users were allowed to develop software programs that were likely to contain errors, or at best inconsistencies in the way in which data were processed. The lack of information element definition, absence of controls over application of data, and inconsistent processing resulted in output reports in which apparently similar information was really not comparable. The management information system turned out to provide only management confusion.

Technical Advantage

C Company had assembled a number of leading scientists in its laboratories. These scientists developed a new method for making distortion-free glass. C delayed in implementing the new process. In the meantime, some C scientists were telling professional acquaintances about their discoveries. A competitor hired away some of the key scientists and shortly thereafter announced a similar process.

Analysis

C failed to establish its rights to the discovery when it did not act to protect the new process, either by a patent or by establishing the process as a trade secret. By delaying application of the innovative business information C increased the probability that the information would leak. Also, by allowing its scientists to discuss the subject, C surrendered some of its rights under law. Generally, a business has an enforceable right to its information provided that the business establishes information value, marks and handles valued information accordingly, and takes prudent action to protect the information. After-the-fact action is never as effective as prior management decisions on information valuation and protection. Whether in paper or electronic form, most business information may turn out to be competitively critical or embarrassing if exposed.

Hot News

H used computers and computer networks extensively. In the course of business, many employees established files accessible from the networks. An employee, giving in to intellectual curiosity, found a way to enter other employees' files. He was able to assemble a dossier on the history and decisions involved in bringing a new product to market. The story appeared in a trade periodical.

Analysis

H did not secure general files on computer networks; this failure was due to H's impatience to use network facilities without regard for security. To some degree it was also the result of employee ignorance or disregard concerning information values. If employees are to have personal computing and/or communications services, individual acceptance of responsibility for protecting the information resource is critically important. And the business must ensure that the network and terminal facilities provide convenient-to-use security elements.

A Freebie

E Company used a service bureau for various specialized processing. Unknown to E, trusted persons at the service bureau had obtained E's passwords. E subsequently discovered that the sensitive business information had been leaked.

Analysis

High-value business information should, if at all practicable, be processed on a business' own computers, operated and controlled by its own employees. Regardless of the security methods used by suppliers of services, a lesser degree of control and a different degree of loyalty must be expected by the information owner when information is processed or stored by an outside firm. This relative lack of control may be the difference between successfully conserving the data and having it exposed or lost. If high-value information must be processed by an outside service, the data owner should explore the alternatives for using encryption, and should ensure that the service provider meets the most stringent security standards. The administrative controls over changes to systems and security mechanisms should provide reasonable assurance that the customer's data will remain inviolate. If the service provider cannot control his own environment, you cannot anticipate security for your information.

Entrepreneur

I Corporation manufactured automated equipment. An ex-employee approached one of I's engineers and proposed that they jointly set up a new business. The basis for the business was to be secret information that I's engineer was to provide. The engineer reported the proposal to I company security. The information was passed and the miscreant arrested.

Analysis

An employee who was well motivated and aware of the value of information avoided what could have become a serious loss to his employer. Formal programs for information resource management and control are useful but the key is in reaching the employees, who are usually in the best position to protect the information. In the end, effective security measures can usually be negated by employee negligence or intentional breach of trust.

Scholarly Study

A university received a grant from T Company to do research into management practices. The people doing the research wrote letters to key employees of T implying that T approved a survey on strategic decisions. Many T employees answered the survey, thus disclosing valuable competitive information.

Analysis

T employee mailing addresses should have been controlled and not made available to the university. But this is often difficult to do because phone directories and the like are easily obtained. A more serious problem is that T employees replied to the survey without concern that this information may not have been authorized. A clearly defined and well-publicized policy as to who may provide information to outsiders is required.

Telegraph

At Z Corporation, a service bureau utility was used to provide message services. Z managers failed to establish control procedures, although the service provider offered security and control methods. Z was greatly embarrassed when parties unknown used the facility to send absurd messages to executives at customer businesses. Although most recognized the messages at best as a practical joke, some accepted the contents at face value.

Analysis

The introduction of facetious, damaging, or confusing information into business information systems is a clever sabotage. Z should have recognized that providing groups of employees access to business systems had inherent dangers and that it was important to establish individual responsibility for use of the message system. Suitable measures were available to avoid a situation such as the one described. But Z's managers didn't think about the potential for information misuse and failed to act prudently.

Ouch

B&B was a law partnership that used a computer in the firm's offices to maintain a reference library, to prepare case materials, and as a word processor. Because of privacy concerns each case was assigned a password. A college intern was hired for the summer months to assist in bringing various case files up to date. The intern's work was unsatisfactory. After being told that his services were no longer required, the temporary employee secretly changed a number of passwords before leaving for another city. B&B had to hire a software specialist to re-establish access to certain files.

Analysis

Damage or loss of information can result from a lack of awareness about system-related controls. Untrusted people should never be allowed access to valued information. If the temporary employee in this case had been a cashier, he would never had been allowed access to funds after having been fired.

The cases described are typical examples of computer misuse. This kind of costly misuse is more common than the million-dollar computer-crime stories in the press. These cases illustrate the importance of management, valuation, and consistent protection of information as a key business resource; these actions should become routine business practice within the general management responsibility called information resource management. A planned and carefully constructed program information conservation attuned to the business requirements is wanted. Such a dispassionate effort is preferable to excessive concern with the technology of computing and publicized, possibly exaggerated, abuses.

Test Cases

These cases are provided for your consideration and analysis.

Case 1

B Corporation provided general engineering consulting services. B operated a large distributed network of computers and terminals. Many B customers were encouraged to use the networks. When interference and loss of data from B's on-line files became apparent, B set up monitors to record all accesses. These monitors showed that unauthorized people were indeed entering the B network and using B's computers.

B had never established concepts of information valuations. Having been founded by an entrepreneur, B's philosophy had been that "we must trust our people."

Case 2

M Ltd. manufactured and sold office equipment. A computer systems analyst (YY) resigned. YY was an excellent analyst/employee and was well liked. Several months later, the manager of the computer systems department investigated a sharp increase in budget charges for the use of computing services. The investigation showed that the increase in charges was due to use on YY's account. YY's password had never been canceled.

YY had gone into the systems consulting business and had used M's computers from a home terminal and dial-up access connections.

Case 3

OP is a widely known computer service bureau with many customers, among them large industrial companies. After several key executives left OP to go to work for other companies, a customer reported apparent tampering with certain data files stored on OP computers. Investigation showed that parties with privileged access to the computer systems had obtained customer passwords from the protected password files. The executives who had left OP all had privileged access.

OP systems stored user passwords in clear text: the passwords were not encrypted. Several lawsuits were filed against OP for failing to protect client information.

Case 4

QJJ Company was in a high-technology business. QJJ had an extensive research and engineering computer network, with most scientists and engineers having professional workstations. One scientist, B, was able to piece together the plans for an important new product by surveying the "public" files kept by other employees on their individual disk stores.

Many of the information reports obtained were identified as protected in the paper-report formats. However, the information elements that went into these reports were not so identified, and in fact many professional workstation users kept copies of hundreds of notations and memos in the network "public" files.

In several recent cases reported in the business press, new product data has leaked to technical publications far in advance of its official release by the owner of the trade secrets.

II | Information Resource Management Checklist

This checklist is a guide to the minimal sequential actions in getting started on information resource management in a medium-to-large-size business. An asterisk indicates essential actions without which the effort will probably be ineffective.

I. Management commitment
   *A. Letter is used from senior officer (preferably CEO) identifying IRM as a management task. This letter accompanied by
   *B. IRM policy establishing minimum IRM requirements, to include
      1. Business information groupings by function, to identify "information owners."
      2. Information classification nomenclature and value criteria.
   C. Corporate IRM management structure and responsibilities. For example:

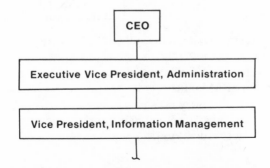

   D. Indoctrination of senior functional managers

      1. Responsibilities as "information owners" for classification, control, safeguarding.

      2. Development of relationships with IRM staff as below.

II. Implementing Actions

  A. Identify company's unique and basic information elements. Establish control requirements through

*B. Functional management (information owner) valuation of information elements and subsequent appropriate classification per policy.

*C. Publish standard on information management, to include

    1. Records conservation

    2. Information security (all forms)

    3. Data administration, to include

      a. Data dictionary

      b. Data-use authorization (per functional information owner)

      c. Database management, including technology, structure, and interfaces for application uses.

    4. Publish implementing organization, for example:

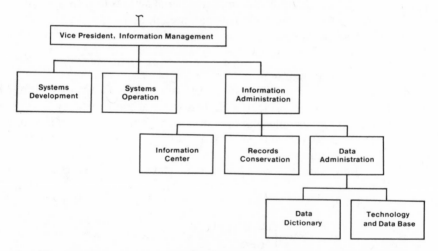

*D. Information science training for all employees working in systems analysis.

III. Establish IRM maintenance and control

  A. Set up plan for IRM audits

  B. Plan for periodic advisory reviews

*C. Assist operating units as appropriate (perhaps mirror image, or via unit security coordinators).

III **Information Resource Management: Policy**

Purpose. To establish operating concepts and minimum requirements for the management and conservation of the information resource.

Responsibilities. The Vice President/Information Management will establish such practices and controls as are required. Operating unit managers will appoint a direct report as information management executive to carry out the information control and conservation activities required.

Scope. All operating units and headquarters worldwide.

Policy. Business information of all types will be controlled and protected as a vital business resource. To accomplish this task

I. All information shall be assigned a value classification as follows:

Registered. Loss or exposure of this information could have serious long-term effects on the operability or profitability of the company. Examples of such information are preannouncement new product data; product-related research findings; unannounced financial summaries; long-range plans; market strategy papers; executive-level personnel decision papers; information required by law to be preserved or shielded.

Private information. Loss or exposure of this information could affect profitability or cause embarrassment to the company. Examples of such information are unit financial plans and results; market or product yearly targets; trade-secret information; competitive survey data; customer lists; product sales reports.

Personal information. Exposure of this information could be regarded as a violation of personal privacy by employees, job applicants, or business contacts. Examples of such information are employee records, employee health records, job-application records, credit records. Also includes any information addressed by privacy legislation.

II. Information shall be managed to provide controls and protection appropriate to the assigned value. At minimum,

Registered information shall be stringently managed to reduce to the minimum vulnerabilities from mishandling, unauthorized exposure, or electronic attack.

Registered documents shall be numbered and controlled by a designated registered librarian at each site. Registered information is to be released to individually named employees only as authorized by the originator or information manager. No copies may be removed from company facilities except through secure couriers assigned by registered librarians.

Registered data shall be stored or transmitted electronically only if encrypted. Registered data may be used in application systems only with the approval of the chief administrative officer.

Private information is to be released only to authorized employee groups who have a specific, job-related need to know. All reasonable effort, as specified in standards, shall be taken to protect private information.

Personal information shall be safeguarded so as to protect the privacy of those individuals concerned, and to meet requirements of all applicable national or local laws.

III. Information management will ensure that business information is organized, conserved, and protected so as to
   A. Minimize information handling and storage costs.
   B. Ensure information reliability, integrity, and privacy.
   C. Meet legal requirements and business contingency needs.
   D. Avoid redundancy and ensure clear definition.
   E. Optimize the use of electronic information technology.

IV. Information management is a subject of special interest for corporate auditors.

IV | Information Resource Management: Standard

Purpose. This standard supplements the policy: Information Management with detailed requirements for the conservation and control of the business information resource. The standard is in sections, as follows:

   I. Information control
  II. Information resource management
 III. Information security
 IV. Information contingency planning
  V. Information retention

Definitions

Information element. The lowest usable level of information—employee name and address; part number. An information element typically occurs within an information *record*; several information records usually constitute a *file*. Information management controls deal with information at the element level, thus constraining information applications at higher levels that are combinations thereof and providing standard data structures and applications interfaces thereto.

Information base. The sum total of all unique, recurring information elements concerning the business of the company. The information base may be in written or electronic form. A third form, mental information, is not directly controllable, but the company may assert legal rights to such information through employee nondisclosure agreements.

Data. Raw or unstructured information; usually but not always the information elements as processed in electronic information systems; the basic information building blocks.

Information Management Structure

All recurring business information shall be catalogued as information elements. The master list of information elements shall become the corporate data dictionary. Operating units may develop operating unit dictionaries but these may not replicate information elements in the corporate data dictionary.

Corporate information management shall

1. Establish value classifications for all information elements.
2. Control the use of information elements by issuing authorities for element use.
3. Ensure that unique corporate information elements are not replicated except as extractions from an authorized information base.
4. Monitor and control information use and applications development to ensure information integrity, reliability, and privacy.
5. Establish information security requirements in line with value classifications assigned.
6. Ensure that business contingency and legal information requirements are satisfied.
7. Establish company legal rights to its information resource through the use of appropriate contracts and agreements, with employees and with outside parties.

Information Control

Business information is to be used only for authorized business purposes. Managers requiring access to business information must be authorized access by information management.

The Vice President/Information Management shall

1. Establish the corporate data base.
2. Establish rules for information use based on information value classifications and policy.
3. Issue authorizations for information access as appropriate to business requirements.
4. Minimize information costs by ensuring proper information application and, avoiding element replication and application redundancies.
5. Analyzing proposed changes to information definitions or information element formats and issue approvals where appropriate.

6. Appoint information managers as appropriate to effect the controls required herein.

Information Resource Management

The Vice President/Information Resource Management is responsible for

1. Identification of information resource requirements in terms of information elements.
2. Determining information resource availability.
3. Fixing logical database-design parameters appropriate to the company's business requirements. In special circumstances this responsibility may be delegated to the unit data resource manager.
4. Approving the software to be used to manage the data base(s).
5. Information-base design, tuning, and control.
6. Ensuring information resource integrity, reliability, and privacy through appropriate security and access authority controls. Provide recovery processes, including data logging and coincident updating control procedures.

Data resource managers shall be appointed in all operating units. The tasks of the data resource managers are:

1. To implement the information control decisions of the information resource manager through the control mechanisms described herein.
2. To minimize information processing costs by establishing and maintaining unique data element configurations and interfaces.
3. To ensure common definition, data element configuration, and codes for interface among operating units and corporate headquarters.
4. To enhance the application of effective information technology. Data management should make business applications independent of information configurations by providing standard interfaces for data element retrieval from the company's information bases. To accomplish this,
   a. A database management system shall be implemented.
   b. The corporate data dictionary shall be complied with, and appropriate additions and modifications recommended to the information resource manager.
   c. Standard data application interfaces shall be designated and used in all systems development activity.
5. The data resource manager shall provide administrative control of the operating unit's information resource by:
   a. Maintaining data dictionaries (as subsets of the corporate data dictionary), database catalog, and schema. Include all current location information, definition status, and access authorities as approved by the information resource manager. (Corporate data elements authorities are reserved.)

b. Interface with company data centers for monitoring of installation and operation of data management software systems.

c. Implement corporate access control rules; provide such operating unit rules as are appropriate to maintain information reliability and integrity.

d. Following corporate information resource manager guidelines for data structure, arrange mapping of information.

e. Participate/advise in decisions on access paths for information retrieval.

V | Information Security Standard

The Vice President/Information Resource Management and the Director/Corporate Security are jointly responsible for devising and implementing programs to ensure the integrity and reliability of the business information base.

Operating unit executive management are responsible for information security requirement compliance.

A. Classification

All information elements will be valued by the assignment of a classification per *policy*. Published material and routine, unsensitive information may not require classification, but are to be considered the property of the company and as such provided reasonable confidentiality.

B. Protection

Protection for company classified information is to be such that *policy* requirements are met or exceeded. Specific details of minimum requirements are in this standard.

C. Business Practices

1. Clean Desk. All business documents, engineering drawings, computer listings, memos, research notebooks, accounting records, and other business records shall be locked away when the work area is unoccupied for two hours or more.

2. Need to know. Authority to retrieve, obtain, see, or possess business information is based on employee job and task assignment. General employee information on company policies and practices, and published information is excepted.

3. Disclosure to outside parties is to be covered by appropriate non-disclosure or contractual agreements, with the advice and approval of the general counsel.

D. All forms of information—written, electronic, mental—are to be controlled and protected. Operating units shall supplement this standard with detailed procedures as needed for strict compliance.

E. Business Operations

1. Valuation Authority. The Vice President/Information Resource Management is the primary authority for information-element valuation and subsequent company classification assignment. This authority is delegated to operating-unit information resource managers for information elements unique to or originating in operating units. Individual employees have classification rights when personal work situation indicates a need; such classifications will be reviewed by the appropriate classification authority as soon as practicable.

2. Marking. All documents, microforms, and electronic media (tapes, disks, cassettes) containing company classified information shall be marked with the classification nomenclature so as to be immediately obvious. At minimum such markings shall be:

For registered information. On cover (required) and on all pages or contents, of a size clearly notable, and including a copy number that is registered with the registered librarian and assigned by name to an authorized employee.

Symbol indicia: `**********************`
                     REGISTERED
                 CONTROL NO._____
                 `***********************`

For private information. On cover and on selected pages (on all content physical items for media) of a size clearly notable.

Symbol indicia: `***********************`
                     PRIVATE
                 `***********************`

For personal information. Same as for private above.

Symbol indicia: `***********************`
                     PERSONAL
                 `***********************`

Note. Computer-generated information media and documents must have program-generated company classification markings except for first-time information or one-time working documents, which may be manually marked. There are no exceptions to this requirement that all company classified items must be appropriately marked to reflect value classification.

3. Handling. Company classified materials must be handled with prudent care in line with the value assigned. At minimum:

Registered information may be distributed, carried, or mailed outside company facilities only by registered librarians. Such transmission must be by registered mail or by courier. Electronic forms may be transmitted over wire or radio only if encrypted from originating station to receiving station, with both stations operated by a registered librarian. Other company classified information is to be distributed as sealed mail or by electronic means that ensure secure delivery to the addressee without exposure. For personal information, a second interior sealed envelope marked with the company classification indicia is required.

Note. Company classification markings are never to be exposed to public view; e.g., markings must never be on outside wrapper of any package or envelope in public mails.

4. Storage. Documents and media are to be stored in line with the valuation classification indicated. At minimum:

Registered: to be stored in a safe or heavy-duty file cabinet with bar lock and combination padlock. Electronic information media may be stored in data-center tape libraries (but not encryption requirement).

Private: to be stored in locked file cabinets or desks. Media stored in large quantities, as in data centers, and the like, must provide positive administrative controls to prevent release of such media to unauthorized persons or for unauthorized uses (such as job setups).

Personal: same as for Private.

Information Security Practices for Employees

It is policy to protect the following information:

Business information

Personal data concerning applicants, employees, and former employees

Proprietary information of suppliers provided under contractual agreement.

Classification.   The internal classification system and uniform practices are for the protection of sensitive business information.

Registered. Information that could cause serious damage to the operation of the company. This is the highest classification and its use and distribution must be strictly limited.

Private. Information that could have a substantially detrimental effect.

Personal. Information of a descriptive, personal nature that a reasonable individual might want to be limited in its disclosure.

Originators of information are responsible for assignment of the appropriate classification.

Handling and marking.   Classified documents are to be marked, distributed, copied, mailed, hand-carried off premises, stored and destroyed only in accordance with prescribed standards.

Program Content

Programs will be implemented to ensure that all employees are advised of their responsibility to protect proprietary information and the reasons for such a requirement. All employees will read and sign the proprietary information and conflict of interest agreement.

Careless talk.   Unnecessary or careless talk about company information must be avoided both on and off the job.

Clean desk.   All employees are to adhere to the clean desk policy. During nonbusiness hours all information must be adequately secured.

Dissemination of information.   Dissemination of information particularly Registered, must be on a need-to-know basis. Need-to-know is a self-imposed discipline. At the heart of this discipline is the determination by the originator and/or the receiver that the information is of intrinsic value to the user and is needed by the user to carry out his or her function.

Disclosure of information.   If, in the course of business, it is necessary that consultants, contractors, and other parties have access to classified material, they must sign a confidential disclosure agreement.

Press relations. Public relations personnel are responsible for dealings with the press. The significance of information to be released must be carefully assessed by the originators beforehand.

Publication Clearance

Wherever the author of any speech, article, presentation or statement, or participant in a panel discussion, outside education programs, or other activity intended for public release is to be identified with the company, clearance must be obtained prior to the publication, delivery, or participation.

Employment advertising for forward technical areas, technical training programs for customers, discussions of technical data with job applicants, organization announcements of components involved in advanced technology, new product development and other sensitive projects, and participation in trade shows and trade association meetings are all subject to prior approval requirements.

Electronic Security

The unique operational characteristics of electronic information make it essential that special security programs be implemented. These are specified in Electronic Security Standards.

Information Security

Clean desk. A clean desk as a practical application for employees is as follows:

> *Business hours.* During absences from the workstation estimated to be in excess of two (2) hours, all classified information is to be removed from the desk and stored in an orderly fashion.

> *Nonbusiness hours.* All information, *classified or not*, is to be removed from the desk and stored in an orderly fashion.

Engineering drawings. All drawings and related documents, regardless of whether or not they are classified, are considered proprietary and must be protected accordingly.

Meetings, conferences, and demonstrations. The chairman or manager convening a meeting, conference, or demonstration at which classified information will be discussed is responsible to:

1. Assure that the people have a need to know the information.
2. Take reasonable precautions.
3. Caution the participants not to carry the discussion beyond the conference room.
4. Assure that no classified documents are left in the conference room during adjournments and upon conclusion of the meeting.
5. Make certain that all visual-aid materials used in a presentation contain the appropriate classification.

Telegrams. Classified information must not be transmitted via overseas or domestic public wire service unless encrypted or masked.

Telephone. Positive identification of the caller and assurance that the caller has a need to know the information that has to be discussed must be established prior to discussing any information over the telephone.

Classification Guidelines

Overclassification must be avoided to prevent unnecessary restrictions, undue costs, and degradation of security by sheer volume. The combination of data contained in a given physical storage device may warrant classification higher than that of its individual record components. When letters of transmittal are attached to classification documents, they must be classified at the same level. The records management program should set retention schedules so that the schedules incorporate the appropriate classification. Security provisions must be commensurate with the sensitivity of the information to be safeguarded.

Authority

The author of the information is primarily responsible for classification of information. If necessary, consult with information resource management or managers of appropriate functional activities. Local security offices will provide assistance.

Downgrading

Experience has shown that many sensitive documents lose their sensitivity after the happening of an event or the passage of time. Downgrading and/

or declassification instructions should be determined and noted when the document is classified.

Classification

Private data. Private data should be used where an unauthorized disclosure would have a substantially detrimental effect on the operation of the company:

1. Could result in the loss of customers.
2. Would be valuable to competitors.
3. Could affect the short-term profitablity.
4. Could reveal technology.

Registered.

1. Registered should be used where serious damage to the company could result from unauthorized disclosure.
   a. Financial information that could result in severe favorable or unfavorable financial reaction.
   b. Information of significance with relation to litigation.
   c. Information that would be of value to competitors' marketing strategies.
2. No more than 1 percent of classified documents should qualify for the Registered classification.

Personal. Personal data is information of a sensitive, personal nature that a reasonable individual might want to be limited in its disclosure. Typical information: employment applications, reference checks, interview evaluations, performance appraisals, correspondence related to salary actions, medical records.

Marking

Registered.

> *Stamps.* Stamps will be issued by the local information management office. Department manager (or equivalent) approval is required.

> *Marking.* The top of each page must be marked.

Transmittal Letters. Must be classified at the same level as the attachment.

Preprinted. Forms and reports may be preprinted with the classification designation to reduce marking effort.

Microfiche. Marked on container and on the heading line in a form visible to the naked eye.

Working Drafts. Working drafts of documents to be classified as Registered may be marked Working Draft—Registered with a stated expiration date. These copies may be distributed only within a *closed work group*.

Registered Numbers. Each copy of the document is numbered. At a minimum, copy number must be entered on the cover, front and back covers of the document, and the title page.

Distribution

Private and personal.   Original and any subsequent distribution must be on a need-to-know basis.

Registered.   Distributed on a need-to-know basis and must have approval of the author and department manager or above. Distribution to exceed 25 addresses requires approval of Vice President/Information Management.

Copying

Copying of nontechnical Private may be authorized at the area manager or higher management level.

Registered.   Copying not authorized. Copies must be obtained directly from a registered librarian.

Personal.   May be copied with approval of the originator.

Mailing

Private.

External. Must be enclosed in two opaque envelopes. Inner envelope sealed, stamped or labeled Private, and marked "open by addressee or designee only."

Internal. Must be enclosed in an opaque envelope that is sealed and marked "open by addressee or designee only."

Registered.

External. Must be enclosed in two opaque envelopes. Inner envelope sealed, stamped or labeled Registered, and marked "open by addressee or designee only."

Internal. Must be enclosed in inner opaque envelope that is sealed, stamped or labeled Registered. Outer envelope may be standard interoffice envelope when sent via internal mail service.

Personal.

External. Must be enclosed in two opaque envelopes.

Internal. Must be enclosed in one opaque envelope that is sealed and stamped or labeled Personal.

Carrying Material Off Premises

Registered material may not be carried off premises. See registered librarian. Sound judgment must be used for other classifications to ensure that protection is maintained.

Electronic Message Systems

Access management requirements per systems standard must be met.

Telex Systems

These systems are not secure and are not to be used for classified information.

Storage

Private and Personal. Must be filed or stored in a locked desk or file cabinet.

Registered. Must be filed or stored in a secure container or safe that is locked nightly. If stored in file cabinet, must be equipped with bar and lock.

Destruction

Private and personal. Burn, shred, or otherwise effectively destroy.

Registered. Burn, shred, or otherwise effectively destroy (registered librarian only).

Mail Distribution

Cleared facilities. Mail centers that handle government classified mail will adhere to the requirements set forth in the U.S. Industrial Security Manual.

Post office. Mail service management will provide the post office with a roster of authorized employees.

Vehicles. Drivers of vehicles picking up or delivering mail will proceed directly to a mail center. No passengers other than employees are to be transported. A vehicle used to transport mail must be locked when the driver leaves the vehicle at any time. If payroll or other checks have to be transported from a check-preparation location, a lockable container should be used. In-plant vehicles used for mail delivery will have a wire cage or other suitable secured enclosure for mail.

Certified, registered mail. Mail centers will maintain a log and record receipt of certified, registered, insured or otherwise controlled mail. Government cleared facilities will handle certified and registered mail in accord with the U.S. Industrial Security Manual.

VI | Electronic Security Standard

I. Managers must control employee use of computing and electronic information systems.

  A. These responsibilities shall be met by using various administrative controls, to include budget controls; monitoring of employee authorizations and computer use; and ensurance of password changes at suitable intervals.

  B. In addition, managers must take prompt action to cancel or change employee authorizations for computer access upon separation or job change.

II. Electronic Security Coordinators are responsible for advising on all matters concerning electronic security policies, standards, and operations, and shall establish working liaison with unit physical security functions.

  A. All employees have a personal responsibility for the protection of company information including that which involves the use of computers or electronic information processing devices.

  B. Employees may not use company computing or electronic information resources for purposes other than authorized.

    1. Electronic Security Implementation—electronic security measures are defined as falling into three levels: physical, procedural, and logical. Within each level are an unlimited number of security elements, the basic building blocks for constructing a protective barrier. Examples of the security levels and their constituent elements are:

    Physical level: door locks, guards, television monitors, trespass alarm systems, digital entry control systems.

Procedural level: records concerning employee authorizations to access computers, monitoring of computer-use logs, inspection of visitor logs, inspection of system software changes, administrative controls over changes to system documentation or application programs.

Logical level: software programs and hardware functions that allow for the identification and authentication of system users, software that scans authorization tables to control user activity, software that provides general control of system penetration, and software or hardware that allows encryption of information.

The combination of security elements necessary to control end-user access to computing resources is called access management:
a. Identification of an individual through something the individual knows, has, or is—usually a claim of identity through the use of a unique code, such as a log-on ID.
b. Authentication, or proof of the identity claimed, by means of a secondary identification token such as password, fingerprint, voiceprint, answer to question.
c. Authorization, the specifying of the actions that the identified, authenticated individual is permitted; the employee may be allowed to see certain data, to run programs, to move or change data or combinations thereof.
All three access management functions are necessary to protect security of information. Further, an administrative function is necessary to maintain access management systems, as described above under I. Managers.
2. Practice—to achieve effective and efficient access management, the following application is required:
a. Identification and Authentication
(1) A unique user identifier (log ID) must be assigned to each employee or contractor employee authorized use of computing resources.
(2) Password changes will be required (by system or by administrative process) per this standard. Where possible, users should be restricted from re-establishing current passwords.
(3) Where possible, passwords will be stored in the system in one-way encrypted form.
b. Authorization—when users are authorized access to company classified information the system must establish positive individual user responsibility by limiting access (need to know) and providing records that support audit trails.
c. Operations—the process of using the access management

system shall be the equivalent of the following, consistent with standard security software or systems requirements.

(1) The computer invites log-on or similar and provides a password blot, if applicable.

(2) User enters identification (log ID) and password or other authentication token.

(3) The system allows only ten or fewer unsuccessful attempts and then requires restart. The computer logs the invalid attempt.

(4) The computer system will control the end-user activity by reference to list of objects (files) and a level of access (read/copy, update, create/delete, execute), established by the Information Resource Manager.

(5) Electronic devices in active mode that are left unattended for two hours (consistent with clean-desk policy) will require procedural or automated monitoring. Where possible, the system should require reauthentication by the user before processing is restarted.

III. Systems Development

To ensure, by proper design, development, and operation, the security of all data used in applications within the company, whether developed for multiuser or personal use.

A. Requirements

Information management is responsible for assisting user in meeting requirements for the protection of information.

Distributed processing systems must be designed so as to ensure that information is protected to a level commensurate with its value classification at all points in the network.

Access management controls must be established for a system that ensures personal responsibility and restricts usage to only those authorized employees who have a need to know to perform assigned tasks.

The protection measures described apply to all computer systems development activities. For small applications, the analyst or programmer must use discretion in selecting a reasonable, effective menu of security measures.

1. Project Initiation

Extraordinary risks should be identified during this phase. Pay particular attention to systems areas that could expose critical data such as advanced product-design information, product launch data, and major program financial information. Make a business decision and write a statement of necessary security requirements.

2. Project Definition

User must make a preliminary determination as to what classification all systems data must have.

3. Analysis and Planning

Potential risks and exposures shall be documented and costed.

4. Design

Controls must be included in the design to ensure data integrity and security. Through a series of processes, these controls automatically call attention to errors or attempts at unauthorized actions and capture information to establish personal responsibility.

   System designers must advise the user on appropriate security measures based on the data classification.

   a. Access Control Systems that require a person or program requesting access to information to offer identification and to authenticate such identity claim.

   b. User Authorization Systems that authorize a user to access only specific data, and/or carry out specific tasks depending on the user's job needs.

   c. Encryption Systems that provide the necessary protection, through encoding, for Registered information during transmission or while stored on magnetic media.

   d. Database Systems and/or application systems accessing data bases must be provided with journalizing or logging and recovery subsystems and function and/or penetration-limiting controls.

5. Procedure Development Including Programming

The detailed development activities for the system must include:

   a. Simple, modular program construction and limitation of programs to reasonable length are important to security.

   b. All testing shall be accomplished via base-case data developed for that purpose.

   c. Computer programs shall be fully documented during the development phase. Documentation must be stored in a secure environment and limited to those employees requiring such information. Where documentation is classified, protection requirements are the same as for other classified documents.

   d. Access management (passwording) must restrict programmer file access to that necessary to accomplish the programmer's assigned duties. Responsibility for administering programmer access shall be specifically assigned.

   e. System procedures must specify the checks and balances provided by the system to maintain information integrity. Procedures must explain how the checks and balances work, when they are to be used, and who is to use them. Any required separation of duties must be specified.

f. Systems implementation documentation must provide detailed instructions for the administration of access controls authorizations and other security functions.

g. Should an application or systems failure occur, restart and recovery procedures and programs must ensure that integrity and security of information is maintained.

h. Contingency planning must be done. Responsible management must be aware of exposures and risks where contingency planning cannot satisfactorily cover exposure.

i. Each system must have procedures to control all changes to the application operating environment, including changes to manual processing, output processing, forms, data center run books, or other operating documentation. Such controls must provide for approvals by system users, systems management, and the data center.

j. Before programs process production data, the user shall be advised of any security requirements defined by this standard that are not in place.

6. Ongoing Support

Procedures shall be defined for handling emergency system changes. They must ensure adequate approvals after the fact, but before such changes become permanent or are applied a second time.

Before application changes are installed as part of the permanent operating environment, management must approve and authorize all program changes through formal sign-off by both the system user and Information Resource Manager. Such approval shall assure continuing security.

Data Centers/Communications Centers

a. At minimum, provide the level of security required for private data. Additional mandatory security protection may be established as appropriate for operating circumstances.

b. Establish and maintain a range of security elements from each level of protection, sufficient to allow users a combination of elements suitable to the company classification of the information processed.

c. Provide a description of available security features for the use of users.

d. Ensure that security appropriate to the company classification of the information processed is maintained consistently throughout networks and distributed processing systems.

e. Environmental

(1) Establish positive physical access control systems that limit entry to authorized employees or authorized (and escorted) visitors.

(2) Establish within the facilities, as appropriate, controlled areas to which access is further restricted to specific employees and visitors: magnetic media storage, contingency vaults, computer processing, job staging and reports printing.

(3) Protect company classified information from casual observation at all times.

7. Operational

   a. Exercise control over and ensure prior approval for all of the following:

     (1) Operating system maintenance

     (2) Hardware maintenance action

     (3) Initial processor loading or equivalent

     (4) Setting of system clocks

     (5) Changes to operating documentation such as runbooks, job tickets, and processing instructions

   b. Ensure sequential numbering (or equivalent control) of all systems logs and console logs to provide an auditable record of all operator actions.

IV. Microcomputers, minicomputers, office systems

All employees are responsible for the protection of company information, including:

A. Using company computers, networks, and services for processing only company business information; any other use must be specifically authorized.

B. Maintaining appropriate security for the workplace by:

   1. Securing the workplace when not attended (clean-desk policy)

   2. Not leaving an active workstation/terminal unattended

   3. Protecting classified company information from casual display

   4. Keeping access management tokens (passwords and the like) private

   5. Protecting, storing, and controlling classified company data, reports, media, and documentation.

C. Maintaining appropriate security for electronic information by:

   1. Changing passwords at least quarterly (more frequently for security administrators and other sensitive jobs)

   2. Not storing or transmitting Registered information unless encrypted

   3. Ensuring that the appropriate company classification is included with electronic messages and files.

D. Protecting documents and storage media by:

    1. Marking output documents and media containers (such as diskette jacket or tape reel) with the appropriate classification.

    2. Not sending or transmitting classified information to nonsecure or nonattended areas.

    3. Ensuring that any outside transfer of media containing company classified information is via courier, insured express, sealed mail, or equivalent.

    4. Applying inventory and recordkeeping methods that will allow prompt identification and location of all media via appropriate marking and storage.

E. Reporting any actual or suspected misuse of such systems to the security coordinator.

F. Managers shall provide organizational and administrative controls that:

    1. Ensure employee understanding of information security requirements.

    2. Promptly cancel or change a terminated/transferred employee's access to company information and facilities.

    3. Provide controls for computers or electronic information-processing equipment.

      a. Establish control through prior approval of all operating system maintenance actions, hardware maintenance actions, all setting of systems clocks, and changes to operating documentation (run books, processing instructions, etc..)

      b. Provide a system log or other control to ensure a complete and auditable review of all actions.

      c. Publish for all users a description of user-selectable security features.

    4. Plan for contingency actions to minimize disruption and ensure recovery in the case of short-term interruptions or a long-term disaster.

    5. Arrange for sharing of sensitive responsibilities if such can result in a security risk. For example, the same person should not be doing programming, operation of equipment, and software maintenance for systems containing classified company information.

    6. Establish unique accountability for each system user: a password must not be used by more than one person.

    7. Assign an administrator, with responsibility for security, for all multiuser systems, to:

      a. Monitor system activities and provide corrective action when violations occur

      b. Maintain access-management control, including installation of accounts, and ensure periodic password changes

       c. Provide backup/recovery of system files/servers

       d. Ensure secure storage of magnetic media, system software, and documentation.

  G. Physical security controls will be established as follows:

    1. Where computing equipment is housed in special facilities:

       a. Require positive identification and authorization before allowing entry to controlled areas.

       b. Provide for escort of visitors.

    2. If classified company information is processed, provide additional protection:

       a. Physically shield devices that display the information, to prevent casual observation.

       b. Enforce procedures for controlling or degaussing/erasing classified company media before scrap or transfer.

       c. Provide containers for classified waste materials.

V. Outside Services and Connections

To ensure consistent protection of company information when such information is processed in computers operated by others, when outsider's software and/or services are used in the processing of company information, and when company-operated computers or electronic information-processing devices are directly connected with such devices not under our control.

  A. Requirements

    1. Registered Information

       a. Registered information may be processed only on company-operated computers in company-controlled facilities. Registered information may not be transmitted to outside locations, computers, or other devices.

       b. The use of outside-developed software and/or outside contract labor or consultants for handling or processing Registered information is not permitted.

    2. Use of Outside Facilities or Processing Services

       Private and/or Personal information may be processed on computers managed and controlled by outsiders only with exception approval by the Vice President/Information Resource Management.

      Further, all requirements of paragraph B.2., immediately following, apply.

       Special care must be taken to ensure that the supplier's facility offers security equivalent to that which would be provided for such classified information in our facility.

       a. Annual security review of the service supplier's facility and procedures for security shall be provided by the Information Resource Manager.

b. Controls (electronic and procedural) will be established to ensure the security of information at all times while in transit or in process.

c. Electronic connections with outside parties—information-processing systems that include or consist of electronic connections between company-controlled computers or electronic devices and computers or devices controlled by others (including dial-up telephone connections), require exception approval. Normal telecommunications service arrangements with public utilities (such as voice/data connections with network switching computers) are excluded from this requirement.

d. Connections as described will be implemented only after:

   (1) Analysis of the potential vulnerabilities of such connections in terms of possible misuse (accidental or purposeful).

   (2) Careful construction of defensive procedure and/or security software that will positively screen outside users from any and all data not intended for their use.

   (3) A formal review and test of such protective measures by a third party (audit or corporate security) prior to system implementation.

   (4) Provision of complete user instructions that implement reasonable security controls (outside user requirements for password changes, notification of user personnel changes, password privacy requirements, user electronic security responsibility assignment, and the like).

   (5) Annual security reviews of such arrangements by the prime user or designee.

VI. Management Approval of Risk Acceptance

To establish a procedure for management approval when unusual risk arises and/or alternatives to policy standards appear appropriate in light of business requirements.

A. Risk Acceptance Approval (RAA) Request shall be processed when:

   1. Business requirements make a limited acceptance of risk through alternative protection measures preferable to the costs of complying with this standard.

   2. Unusual or severe risks are involved in a proposed system or connection.

   3. Supplier premises, computers, or services are to be used to process company classified information.

   4. Connections are to be established directly between company-controlled computers or devices and computers or devices con-

trolled by others (except in the case of connection with public
utility computer switches or facilities for telecommunications
voice and data services).
B. Requests for RAA must be processed as follows:
   1. For systems handling Registered information:
     a. A formal risk analysis must be provided, considering
       (1) the operating environment
       (2) vulnerabilities and risks
       (3) potential effect should an attack be successful
       (4) comparison of costs of the alternative protection meas-
          ures proposed and compliance with this standard.
     b. Vice President/Information Resource Management must
       concur.
     c. An operating unit president must approve in writing.
   2. For systems handling Private or Personal information:
     a. An analysis justifying the exception must be provided, in-
       cluding a comparison of the costs of the proposed protection
       methods versus the costs of complying with this standard.
     b. An operating unit vice president must approve in writing.
   3. For systems processing unclassified information:
     A request for approval, including risk/benefits analysis, must
     be approved by the operating unit information resource manager.

VII | Computer-Crime Legislation Proposal (Draft: State of Connecticut, 1983)

An Act Concerning Computer Related Offenses

Be it enacted by the Senate and House of Representatives in General Assembly convened:

Section 1.   (NEW) (a) For the purposes of this act:

(1) "Access" means to instruct, communicate with, store data in, or retrieve data from a computer, computer system or computer network.

(2) "Computer" means a programmable, electronic device capable of accepting and processing data.

(3) "Computer network" means (A) a set of related devices connected to a computer by communications facilities, or (B) a complex of two or more computers, including related devices, connected by communications facilities.

(4) "Computer program" means a set of instructions, statements or related data that, in actual or modified form, is capable of causing a computer or computer system to perform specified functions.

(5) "Computer services" includes, but is not limited to, computer access, data processing and data storage.

(6) "Computer software" means one or more computer programs, existing in any form, or any associated operational procedures, manuals, or other documentation.

(7) "Computer system" means a computer, its software, related equipment, communications facilities, if any, and includes computer networks.

(8) "Data" means information of any kind in any form, including computer software.

(9) "Person" means a natural person, corporation, trust, partnership, incorporated or unincorporated association and any other legal or governmental entity.

(10) "Private personal data" means data concerning an individual which a reasonable person would want to keep private and which is protectable under law.

(11) "Property" means anything of value, including data.

(b) Unauthorized access to a computer system.

(1) A person is guilty of the computer crime of unauthorized access to a computer system when, knowing that he is not authorized to do so, he accesses or causes to be accessed any computer system without authorization.

(2) It shall be an affirmative defense to a prosecution of unauthorized access to a computer system that:

(A) The actor reasonably believed that the owner of the computer system, or a person enpowered to license access thereto, had authorized him to access; or

(B) The actor reasonably believed that the owner of the computer system, or a person empowered to license access thereto, would have authorized him to access without payment of any consideration; or

(C) The actor reasonably could not have known that his access was unauthorized.

(c) Theft of computer services. A person is guilty of the computer crime of theft of computer services when he accesses or causes to be accessed a computer system with the intent to obtain unauthorized computer services.

(d) Interruption of computer service. A person is guilty of the computer crime of interruption of computer services when he, without authorization, intentionally or recklessly disrupts or degrades or causes the disruption or degradation of computer services or denies or causes the denial of computer services to an authorized user of a computer system.

(e) Misuse of computer system information. A person is guilty of the computer crime of misuse of computer system information when

(1) As a result of his accessing or causing to be accessed a computer system, he intentionally makes or causes to be made an unauthorized display, use, disclosure or copy, in any form, of data residing on, communicated by, or produced by a computer system; or

(2) He intentionally or recklessly and without authorization

(A) alters, deletes, tampers with, damages, destroys, or takes data intended for use by a computer system, whether residing within or external to a computer system, or

(B) intercepts or adds data to data residing within a computer system; or

(3) He knowingly receives or retains data obtained in violation of Section (e) (1) or (2); or

(4) He uses or discloses any data he knows or believes was obtained in violation of Section (e) (1) or (2).

(f) Destruction of computer equipment. A person is guilty of the computer crime of destruction of computer equipment when he, without authorization, intentionally or recklessly tampers with, takes, transfers, conceals, alters, damages or destroys any equipment used in a computer system or causes the foregoing to occur.

Section 2.   (NEW) (a) (1) Any aggrieved person who has reason to believe that any other person has been engaged, is engaged or is about to engage in an alleged violation of Section 1 may bring an action against such person and may apply to the superior court for the following:

(A) any order temporarily or permanently restraining and enjoining the commencement or continuance of such act or acts;

(B) an order directing restitution;

(C) an order directing the appointment of a receiver. Subject to making due provisions for the rights of innocent persons, a receiver shall have the power to sue for, collect, receive and take into his possession any property which belongs to the person alleged to have violated Section 1 and which may have been derived by, used in or aided in any manner any computer crime. The types of property covered by this section shall include: all the goods and chattels, rights and credits, moneys and effects, books, records, documents, papers, choses in action, bills, notes and property of every description including all computer system equipment and data, and including property with which such property has been commingled if it cannot be identified in kind because of such commingling; the receiver shall also have the power to sell, convey, and assign all of the foregoing and hold and dispose of the proceeds thereof under the direction of the court. Any person who has suffered damages as a result of a violation of Section 1, and submits proof to the satisfaction of the court that he has in fact been damaged, may participate with general creditors in the distribution of the assets to the extent he has sustained out-of-pocket losses. The court shall have jurisdiction of all questions arising in such proceedings and may make such orders and judgments therein as may be required.

(2) The court may award the relief applied for or such other relief as it may deem appropriate in equity.

(b) Independent of or in conjunction with an action under section (a), any person who suffers any injury to person, business or property may bring an action for damages against a party who is alleged to have violated Section 1. The aggrieved party shall recover actual damages and damages for unjust enrichment not taken into account in computing damages for actual loss and treble damages where there has been a showing of willful and malicious conduct.

(c) The Attorney General may institute proceedings under this section.

The commencement of proceedings by the Attorney General shall not affect the rights of aggrieved persons independently to pursue civil remedies.

(d) Proof of pecuniary loss is not required to establish actual damages in any action arising under this act and concerning the unauthorized access to or misuse of private personal data.

(e) In civil actions against a person who is found to have violated Section 1, whether at law or in equity, the court shall award to any aggrieved person who prevails, reasonable costs and reasonable attorney's fees.

(f) The filing of a criminal action against a defendant is not a prerequisite to a civil action under this Chapter.

(g) No action under Section 2 may be brought but within three years from the date the computer crime is discovered or should have been discovered by the exercise of reasonable diligence.

Section 3.   (NEW) (a) A person is guilty of computer crime in the first degree when he is found to have violated Section 1 and the damage to or the value of the property or services exceeds $10,000. Computer crime in the first degree is a Class B felony.

(b) A person is guilty of computer crime in the second degree when the damage to or the value of the property or services exceeds $5,000. Computer crime in the second degree is a Class C felony.

(c) A person is guilty of computer crime in the third degree when the damage to or the value of the property or services exceeds $1,000 or he recklessly engages in conduct which creates a risk of serious personal injury to another person. Computer crime in the third degree is a Class D felony.

(d) A person is guilty of computer crime in the fourth degree if the damage to or the value of the property or services does not exceed $1,000. Computer crime in the fourth degree is a Class A misdemeanor.

(e) A person is guilty of computer crime in the fifth degree if the damage to or the value of the property or services does not exceed $500. Computer crime in the fifth degree is a Class B misdemeanor.

(f) Alternative fine based on defendant's gain. If a person has gained money, property or services or other consideration through the commission of any felony or misdemeanor under this Chapter, upon conviction thereof the court, in lieu of the fine fixed by this section, may sentence the defendant to pay an amount, fixed by the court, not to exceed double the amount of the defendant's gain from the commission of the offense. In such case the court shall make a finding as to the amount of defendant's gain from the offense, and if the record does not contain sufficient evidence to support such a finding, the court may conduct a hearing upon the issue. For the purpose of this section, the term "gain" means the amount of money or the value of property or services or other consideration derived.

(g) Amounts included in violations of Section 1 committed pursuant to one scheme or course of conduct, whether from the same person or several persons, may be aggregated in determining the grade of the offense.

(h) Classification of computer related crimes. Any person who conspires to commit, attempts to commit or causes another to commit any offense within this part shall be punished as though he had committed the crime.

Section 4. (NEW) Miscellaneous.

(a) Value of property or services. For the purpose of this Chapter, the value of property or services shall be ascertained as follows:

(1) Except as otherwise specified in this Chapter, value means the greater of

(A) the market value of the services or property at the time of the crime; or

(B) if the services or property is unrecoverable, damaged or destroyed as a result of a violation of Section 1, the cost of reproducing or replacing the services or property at the time of the violation.

(2) When the value of the services or property or damage thereto cannot be satisfactorily ascertained, the value shall be deemed to be not less than $250.

(b) Situs of offense. If any act performed in furtherance of the offenses set out in this part occurs in this state or if any computer system or part thereof accessed in violation of this part is located in this state, the offense shall be deemed to have occurred in this state.

(c) Provisions of this Chapter not exclusive. The provisions of this Chapter shall be applied in addition to any penal or other law of this state which applies or may apply to any transaction in violation of this Chapter. The provisions of this Chapter shall be broadly construed. They shall not, however, be construed to create legal or equitable rights equivalent to any of the exclusive rights within the general scope of United States copyright and patent laws, but shall be construed to the extent possible to provide remedies in addition thereto.

# VIII | **Automated Logical Access Control Standard***

Objective

To enforce an optimum set of logical access controls to confidential data and text for the purposes of maintaining adequate security.

Scope

Any computer whose use is shared by a closed community of users, any of whom may use the computer directly via terminals for certain pre-authorized purposes.

Where the data or text which are held are either

confidential to the organization or part of the organization using the computer and/or

subject to other need-to-know restrictions, e.g., for internal control reasons, personal privacy, etc.

Terminology

In this standard the word "computer" is used to encompass any computer, (sub-) system, shared intelligent workstation, or group thereof, with which a user communicates in interactive or batch mode, and which is a separate entity from a security control viewpoint.

Requirements

The following minimum requirements must be met. For each requirement the corresponding security objective is given alongside:

* By Charles R. Symons and James A. Schweitzer. From *Proceedings of the Second International Congress and Exposition on Computer Security*. Amsterdam: North Holland Publishing Co., 1984; reprinted with permission.

Requirement	*Security Objective*

A. *UserID.* A UserID, minimum six characters must be assigned to each individual user; which is unique to that computer. The computer will not allow two or more terminals to be signed on simultaneously with the same UserID.

Inhibits sharing of UserID's, and emphasizes individual accountability for usage and security.

Although assigned to an individual person, a UserID may belong to one or more recognized groups of UserID's which share common access authorizations (see C.2 a, below).

Helps simplify administration of access authorizations.

B. *Passwords.* Each individual UserID must have an associated password which the User is instructed to keep private with the following characteristics:

Password is the key to authenticating that the user is indeed the individual identified by the UserID.

1. *Length.* minimum of 6 alpha-numeric or special characters, excluding blanks.

Makes password harder to guess by trial-and-error.

2. *Frequency of change.* The computer will force a password to be changed within D days of the last change, where D is an installation parameter with maximum 99 days, default 30 days.

Forced password changing reduces the security exposure if an existing password has become known to other persons than the password-owner. Forced changing also heightens general user security consciousness.

3. *Repeatability.* The computer will maintain a list of the last P passwords used by the UserID and will not accept an attempt to change to a password already used and still in the list. P is an installation parameter with a minimum of 10 passwords.

Inhibits the user trying to beat the enforced password changing control.

4. *Initialization.* When a new UserID is established it will be given an "expired" password (see C.1 c, below), that is one which must be changed at the first attempted sign-on by the UserID.

Prevents the person allocating UserID's from knowing the password which will be used by the user concerned.

5. *Encryption.* All passwords will be stored in the computer in one-way

Prevents a system programmer or someone working in "privileged" mode (see encrypted form. A password entered during an interactive sign-on or a batch job submission will be immediately encrypted at the time of entry, and thereafter never displayed in clear text.

C.3, below) from obtaining passwords and thereby being able to impersonate any UserID.

C. *Logical Access Control*

1. *Sign-on (Identification/Authentication) Phase.*

Sign-on will follow the procedure below, from the point where the computer is ready to accept identification of the user via a UserID.

a. Computer invites sign-on, by requesting entry of the UserID. If accepted the computer proceeds with step b. If not accepted the computer allows up to two more attempted entries, and then if still unsuccessful:
   (1) logs all unsuccessfully tried UserID's
   (2) alerts Operator or System Security Administrator
   (3) (if appropriate) disconnects the terminal.

Procedure is designed to help the genuine user, but inhibit someone trying to find an acceptable UserID by trial-and-error.

b. Computer invites entry of password, and provides a "blot" (or inhibits display or printing). User enters password, and if successful, the computer proceeds with step c. If unsuccessful the computer allows up to two more attempted entries, and if still unsuccessful:
   (1) logs all unsuccessfully tried passwords
   (2) alerts Operator or System Security Administrator
   (3) (if appropriate) disconnects the terminal.

Procedure is designed to help the genuine user, but inhibit someone trying to guess a password by trial-and-error.

N.B. The computer should enforce a time delay of minimum two seconds between repeated attempted entries of a password.

Inhibits someone successfully using a computer to generate passwords systematically to gain entry.

c. The computer checks if today the password is more than E days from the date of expiry (E is an installation parameter, usually set to 20% of the forced change period D). If the password is still more than E days from the expiry, the computer proceeds with step f.

To be as helpful as possible the computer gives advance warning to a user whose password is due to expire imminently.

d. If the password is within E days of expiry, but still unexpired, the computer issues a warning giving the number of days remaining before the password must be changed. Alternatively, if the password expires today, or is already expired, the computer informs the user that the password must be changed immediately.

e. The computer issues an invitation to change the password, indicating the format, and supplying a "blot" (or inhibiting display or printing). The user may ignore the invitation to change by pressing "Return" unless the password is already expired, or expires today. If the user enters a new password, the computer invites a repeat entry to validate the first entry, and continues until two successive identical passwords are entered.

The computer helps the user change password, and enforces change of an expired password. A changed password is requested a second time to avoid problems which would be caused by a typing error during the first entry, and to reinforce the new password in the user's memory.

f. The computer issues a message stating the date and time when the last successful sign-on was made.

Provides a check for the user that his UserID has not been used without the user's knowledge.

Batch Job or message submission from an interactive terminal or workstation

g. The computer will only allow a batch job or message to be submitted for execution, or sent from an interactive terminal or workstation if the batch job or message is associated with the same UserID/password combination used for initial sign-on.

Prevents a user signing on under one UserID with associated authorizations and then creating and submitting a job with a different authorization.

h. Sign on proceeds essentially as in Interactive mode, except that the computer does not provide guiding messages, and if any step is unsuccessful the job is canceled.

2. *Processing (Authorization) Phase.*

a. Any computer to which the UserID may gain access will control, using information provided by the owner of the "object" concerned:

Each UserID should be limited in what use can be made of the computer by pre-agreed "need-to-know" considerations.

(1) The list of "objects" (programs, transactions, files, etc.) to which the UserID is allowed access either individually or by virtue of membership of a recognized group, or of preregistered attributes.

(2) The "level" of access (read, copy, update, create/delete, execute) allowed to the objects. Additionally the computer will log all attempts to access objects outside the range authorized for the UserID and warn the user (interactive mode) or cancel the job (batch mode).

b. The list of UserID's or recognized groups of UserID's that may access any object, and the associated level of access may only be changed by

The rules and mechanisms for changing access authorizations must be clearly and coherently established; they will vary depending on the type of computing service. Time-sharing and office systems usually

(1) the UserID which individually created the object, or

(2) the object's "owner" (if such is established), or

(3) the System Security Administrator working in Privileged Access mode (see below).

allow only the creator of an object to change the access authorizations. In contrast a community of users sharing a common data base is better regulated via a System Security Administrator acting on behalf of the data base "owner."

c. Any major subsystem executing on the computer which is shared by users with different "need-to-know" requirements, and which is treated as a single "object" by the computer's security system, must itself provide its own authorization scheme along the lines of a above.

The computer's security system may not be able to cope with incompatible security conventions of a "foreign" subsystem. The latter must therefore provide its own authorization mechanisms.

d. If a terminal or workstation is inactive for more than T minutes, the associated UserID will be automatically signed off. T will be an installation parameter with a default of 15 minutes.

Prevents someone using a terminal which has been left by a user who forgot to sign-off.

3. *Privileged Access.*

A privileged access mode will be available to a System Security Administrator for maintenance of all security and logical access control parameters, but only for those purposes. Privileged access will not be needed for any application programming, or use of an application or utility program.

A privileged access mode is essential for security administration, such as establishing and deleting UserID's changing certain types of access authorizations, etc. Such a privileged access mode must itself be protected from unauthorized use to at least the ALACS standard.

4. *Logging.*

All unsuccessful sign-on attempts, and all unsuccessful access attempts during processing will be recorded in a log in the computer concerned, available only in privileged access mode. All log message-types will be uniquely coded, and date and time stamped to enable analysis. Analysis programs will be provided

A log of attempted security violations is an essential defense mechanism to help a System Security Administrator discover apparent deliberate attempted violations.

which highlight suspicious repeat-
edly unsuccessful sign-on or access
attempts.

5. *Authorization Maintenance.*

Administration Procedures will be
established for each computer such
that

Sound procedures to administer UserID's
are an essential counterpart to the com-
puter-enforceable security measures.

a. if an individual leaves the organization any individual UserID
is immediately canceled.

b. if an individual's job is changed,
then any consequential changes
of the individual's authorization
to access programs, transactions, data, etc. are immediately
effected.

D. *Optional Refinements.*

1. *Physical Terminal constrained to
certain UserIDs.* The computer may
allow only certain UserID's to sign-
on to certain physical terminals.

This is a valuable option for situations
where specific computer processing
should be possible only from certain terminals which could be at a specific secure
location, equipped with certain security
features, etc., due to the need to handle
particularly sensitive data.

2. *Dial-up.* An indication of whether
or not access via a dial-up port is
allowed will be associated with
each UserID. An attempt to use
dial-up when not authorized will
result in failure to sign-on.

Anyone wanting to try to obtain a
UserID/password combination by trial-an-
error will probably need the privacy of a
remote dial-up link to make the attempt.
Therefore limiting dial-up access to
known UserID's who have valid reasons
for dial-up can limit the security risk.

3. *Unused UserIDs.* If a UserID is unused for more than say 90 days the
computer logs that fact so that the
System Security Administrator can
ascertain if the UserID is still
needed.

A valuable aid for the System Security
Administrator in isolating potentially de-
funct UserIDs.

IX Glossary

access management (logical)
Control of access to data stored, processed, or communicated electronically, usually by means of hardware and/or software systems.

authentication
Proof of a claimed identity through a secondary token, usually private and secret; typically a password, but may also be a hand measurement, fingerprint, eye-retina scan, encrypted magnetic card, etc.

authorization
The process of permitting an identified and authenticated user to see, move, or modify specified data, or to run a program, according to preauthorized rights or privileges.

contingency planning
The management responsibility that addresses the need for ensuring a continuity of business operation; planning for alternative information sources and backup information processing means in the event of a fire, flood, or man-made disaster.

data
Unformatted, "raw" information that is typically in some organized sequence for machine (computer) processing; most typically, numerical data. Compare *Information.*

electronic information
Data or information in electronically readable forms; usually in digital code.

identification
A claim to be a certain person or program (in a computer process); usually made by offering a primary token, such as a password, account number, identity card, or the like.

information	Data that have been organized for presentation by structuring for appearance or understandability; may be filled out with text for definition or clarification; data in decision form. Compare *data*.
information integrity	The quality of completeness, wholeness, and accuracy; information that is true; information that is exactly as entered to a record or system.
information reliability	The quality of being available when and where needed.
information resource management	The management responsibility and process of organizing, assigning value to, controlling, and generally managing information as a business resource of significant value; IRM.
information security	The provision of protection for information resources so as to ensure their reliability and integrity.
risk management	The management responsibility for determining risk acceptance policy; the process of offsetting business risks with insurance or operating alternatives within a given risk acceptance posture set by management.
security coordinator	An employee with an additional responsibility for monitoring and advising on security matters within that employee's work unit, office, or area.
security elements	Any of various features included in security systems: locks, passwords, keys, barriers, logs or records, codes.
security levels	The three major categories of security elements—physical, procedural, logical.
token	Something a person or program knows, has, or is, which purports to identify that person or program, especially when attempting to access electronic forms of data. Typically a password.

References

1. Brand, Stewart. 1984. *Whole Earth Software Catalog*. New York: Doubleday.
2. Brinberg, Herbert R. 1984. Effective Management of Information: How to Meet the Needs of All Users. *Management Review* (New York: American Management Association) (February).
3. Can You Believe This? 1983. *Computer Security Newsletter* Northborough, Mass.: Computer Security Institute, 50 (January–February): 1.
4. Computer Crime. 1983. *Data Communications* (May): 54.
5. Controlling Distributed Data. 1983. *EDP Analyzer*. September.
6. Diebold, John. 1979. Forward to IRM: New Directions in Management. *Infosystems* (October): 41.
7. Diebold, John. 1982. In Depth. *Computerworld* (July).
8. Domestic Council Committee on the Right to Privacy. 1973. *Report to the President*. Washington, D.C.: National Commission on Libraries and Information Science.
9. Eason, Tom S., and Douglas A. Webb. 1982. *Nine Steps to Effective EDP Loss Control*. Boston: Digital Press. P. 19.
10. Highland, Harold Joseph. 1984. *Protecting Your Microcomputer System*. New York: Wiley.
11. Hoffman, Lance. 1977. *Modern Methods for Computer Security and Privacy*. Englewood Cliffs, N.J.: Prentice-Hall.
12. How the Management Job is Changing. 1984. *EDP Analyzer* (June).
13. Information Systems' New Strategic Role. 1984 (January).
14. Liebholz, S. W., and Louis D. Wilson. 1974. *User's Guide to Computer Crime*. Radnor, Pa.: Chilton. P. ix.
15. Martin, James. 1969. *Security, Accuracy, and Privacy in Computer Systems*. Englewood Cliffs, N.J.: Prentice-Hall. Pp. 249, 357.
16. Merlini, M. 1984. Crime Does Pay for Italy's White Collar Criminals. *Computing (UK)* (January 22): 34.
17. Miller, Arnold. 1983. Time to Light the Torches. *Infosystems* (July): 124.
18. Moyer, James S. 1983. Proper Approach to Information Management. *Infosystems* (May): 72.

19. Naisbitt, John. 1982. *Megatrends*. New York: Warner Books.
20. Nycum, Susan. 1984. Data and Program Ownership and Other Legal Issues. In *Proceedings of the Second International Congress and Exhibition of Computer Security*. Amsterdam: North Holland Publishing Company.
21. Planning Your Distributed Systems. 1983. *EDP Analyzer* (June).
22. Rivest, R., A. Shamir, and L. Adelman. 1977. A Method for Obtaining Digital Signatures and Public Key Cryptosystems. Cambridge, Mass.: MIT Press. LCS/TM82.
23. Rockhart, J. F., Leslie Ball, and Christine V. Bullen. 1982. Future Role of the Information Systems Exeuctive *MIS Quarterly* (special issue).
24. Schweitzer, James A. 1982. *Managing Information Security: A Program for the Electronic Information Age*. Woburn, Mass.: Butterworth.
25. Schweitzer, James A. 1983. *Protecting Information in the Electronics Workplace*. Reston, Va.: Reston Publishing Company.
26. Spanner, Robert A. 1984. *Who Owns Innovation*. Homewood, Ill.: Irwin.
27. Study Cites Lack of Data on EFT Crime. 1983. *Computerworld* (July 18): 12.
28. Symons, Charles R., and James A. Schweitzer. 1984. A Proposal for an Automated Logical Access Control Standard. In *Proceedings of the Second International Congress and Exposition on Computer Security*. Amsterdam: North Holland Publishing Company.
29. Synott, W. R., and W. H. Gruber. 1981. *Information Resource Management*. New York: Wiley. P. 12.
30. U.S. Department of Defense Computer Security Center. 1983. *Trusted Systems Evaluation Criteria*. Washington, D.C.: U.S. Government Printing Office. (CSC 001–83).
31. Vincent, David R. 1984. Information on the Bottom Line. *Computerworld* (August 13): ID125.
32. Wicklein, John. 1981. *Electronic Nightmare*. Boston: Beacon Press. P. 6.

Index

James A. Schweitzer, CDP, is Systems Security
Technology Manager for Xerox Corporation, a
worldwide manufacturer and marketer of office
systems products. Mr. Schweitzer is responsible
for the design, maintenance, and monitoring of
security systems and procedures covering all
Xerox computing and telecommunications activities worldwide. He has special responsibilities for application of security technologies
in the Xerox Research Centers.

Mr. Schweitzer is the author of two books on
computer security management. These are
**Managing Information Security: A Program
for the Electronic Information Age** and
**Protecting Information in the Automated
Workplace: A Guide for Managers.** He is also
Chairman of the Special Interest Group on Secu-
rity, Audit, and Control with the Association for
Computing Machinery, and a member of the
Board of Editors for the journal *Computers and
Security* (North-Holland Publishing Company).

Mr. Schweitzer holds the MBA degree from
Indiana University, and a BS degree in Management from Duquesne University.